T0114822

Vocabulary

The READING PUZZLE

Elaine K. McEwan

Val Bresnahan

CORWIN PRESS
Classroom

For information:

Corwin Press
A SAGE Company
2455 Teller Road
Thousand Oaks, California 91320
CorwinPress.com

SAGE Ltd.
1 Oliver's Yard
55 City Road
London EC1Y 1SP
United Kingdom

SAGE India Pvt. Ltd.
B 1/I 1 Mohan Cooperative
Industrial Area
Mathura Road, New Delhi
India 110 044

SAGE Asia-Pacific Pvt. Ltd.
33 Pekin Street #02-01
Far East Square
Singapore 048763

ISBN: 978-1-4129-5827-1

This book is printed on acid-free paper.

08   09   10   11   12   10 9 8 7 6 5 4 3 2 1

Executive Editor: Kathleen Hex
Managing Developmental Editor: Christine Hood
Editorial Assistant: Anne O'Dell
Developmental Writer: Val Bresnahan
Developmental Editor: Joellyn Cicciarelli
Proofreader: Carrie Reiling
Art Director: Anthony D. Paular
Design Project Manager: Jeffrey Stith
Cover Designers: Michael Dubowe and Jeffrey Stith
Illustrator: Drew Rose
Design Consultant: The Development Source

Vocabulary

The READING PUZZLE

TABLE OF CONTENTS

Introduction

Are you ready to catch students who are "falling through the cracks"? Are you ready to teach them all to read? While it is often easy to identify at-risk students, teaching them can be a challenge. The challenge is often due to critical variables over which teachers have no control, including IQ level, early literacy experiences, socioeconomic status, or the educational level of parents or guardians. The good news is that while you cannot change many things, you can change how you teach. You can instruct in a manner that will enable *all* students to learn.

Because vocabulary has been identified by the National Reading Panel (2000) as one of the critical areas of reading instruction, this book focuses on vocabulary instruction for all students, especially those whose underdeveloped word knowledge negatively impacts their academic performance. This underperformance is characterized by a partial knowledge of word meanings, confusion of words with similar sounds, and limited knowledge of how and when words are typically used. To help at-risk students, several essential instructional factors must be consciously addressed.

The first essential factor for teaching at-risk students is instructional planning and behavior. "Word Selection and Definition" (pages 8–15) helps you choose words and plan for vocabulary instruction. Teaching behaviors are explained in "Take Five" (pages 16–20) and are woven into the remaining sections of this book.

Four additional factors for comprehensive vocabulary teaching are the following: extensive reading, direct instruction of important individual words, teaching word-learning strategies, and fostering word awareness (Feldman & Kinsella, 2002). The remainder of this book addresses each essential factor.

With the help of this resource, you can provide a thorough, well-balanced vocabulary program so that all students are reading and none are left behind.

978-1-4129-5827-1

Put It Into Practice

With the mandate to leave no child behind (No Child Left Behind, NCLB) and the approaching deadline of 2014 for all students to be proficient in reading, school districts and teachers at every grade level are working diligently to improve the reading skills of all students.

The National Reading Panel (2000) identified five areas that increase students' reading ability: phonemic awareness, the alphabetic principle, fluency, vocabulary, and reading comprehension. After third grade, the reading gap is thought to be primarily a vocabulary gap. If students can decode words but still have comprehension difficulties, the culprit is often the inability to understand word meaning—a vocabulary deficit. If students do not know the meaning of the majority (95%) of the words in a paragraph, passage, or story, they will have great difficulty understanding what they are reading.

After the third grade, at-risk students often struggle with less common, more academic words. This vocabulary difficulty affects comprehension and fluency. The result is a downward spiral. Students do not know the meaning of words, so they cannot comprehend what they read. Therefore, they read less and subsequently learn less vocabulary. As a result, students learn less content, and they cannot use the content to glean meaning from unfamiliar words.

Strategies used to increase vocabulary skills are an important part of the Reading Puzzle. The Reading Puzzle is a way of organizing and understanding reading instruction, as introduced in my book, *Teach Them All to Read: Catching the Kid Who Fall Through the Cracks* (2002). The puzzle contains the essential reading skills that students need to master in order to become literate at every grade level. *The Reading Puzzle, Grades 4–8* series focuses on five of these skills: Word Analysis, Comprehension, Fluency, Spelling, and Vocabulary.

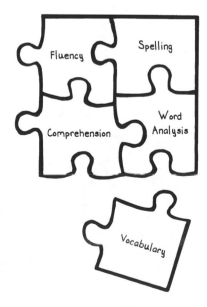

Most upper-grade teachers readily acknowledge the critical importance of teaching vocabulary (McEwan, 2002). Unfortunately, some published programs use inappropriate teaching demonstrations or provide insufficient practice, requiring major modifications to adequately teach vocabulary (Jitendra & Kameenui, 1994). In addition, teachers sometimes omit or reduce vocabulary instruction to "get through the material." Rather than being seen as essential, vocabulary is often considered ancillary, being quickly presented, tested, and forgotten.

Fortunately, classrooms are highly verbal environments. With targeted and direct vocabulary instruction, students with language difficulties, English language learners, economically disadvantaged students, and students with learning disabilities can all become better readers and better all-around students.

This book has been designed to put theory and research into practice and provide students with the targeted and direct vocabulary instruction that they need.

Word Selection and Definition

This section provides you with concrete ways to select vocabulary words and plan lessons.

Take Five

This section includes presentation techniques so you can make the most of each lesson and provide an atmosphere in which all students can learn.

Chapter 1: Extensive Reading Lessons

This chapter focuses on ways for students to improve their vocabulary in a natural way through reading. Because at-risk learners frequently do not read often enough or at the right level of difficulty to acquire word knowledge, they must be explicitly taught how to select books and be encouraged to read. With explicit instruction on book selection and an accountability system, at-risk learners can systematically build vocabulary and increase vocabulary learning in a systematic way.

Chapter 2: Vocabulary Instruction Lessons

This chapter is dedicated to direct instruction of vocabulary words and contains a multitude of cumulative, sequential activities. These activities should be presented in sequence, as one activity builds upon the next. This approach gives at-risk learners repeated practice in a variety of contexts, a required strategy for effective vocabulary acquisition.

I wonder what the word "wrenched" means?

978-1-4129-5827-1

Chapter 3: Strategy Lessons

This chapter provides the best practices of good readers. At-risk learners and struggling readers should be taught these strategies explicitly and in order with repeated practice. Some of these strategies include using context clues, prefixes, suffixes, and word bases to determine meaning.

Chapter 4: Word Awareness Lessons

This chapter focuses on increasing word consciousness. Typically, at-risk learners are not aware of the words around them. They do not pay attention to unfamiliar words while they read or while listening to others speak. This final chapter provides activities to increase word awareness in all language tasks: listening, speaking, reading, and writing. Studies have shown that children's vocabularies increase at a rate of 3,000 words per year or about six to eight words per day (Nagy & Anderson, 1984).

Between third and seventh grade, their vocabularies almost double. This growth cannot be solely developed through direct classroom teaching. It would be impossible to teach that many words. Students need direct experience with oral and written language to achieve this type of growth. They must become enthralled with the words around them. Students learn new words by engaging in conversations with adults, listening to adults read to them, and by reading on their own. Even television can be the source of new vocabulary. Students learn new words on their own when they become fascinated by words.

Word Selection and Definition

Intensive, direct vocabulary instruction is critical to produce in-depth vocabulary knowledge. The first challenge is to decide which words to teach. If you carefully analyze text and provide a rationale for words to be taught, instructional time will be maximized. Well-planned, explicit vocabulary instruction involves conscientious vocabulary preparation.

Utility Check

One proven method to help you determine which words to target for explicit vocabulary instruction is the utility check. As you consider words, analyze them according to their levels of utility, and teach them as suggested below.

Tier I

Tier I words are basic words that commonly appear in spoken language and in numerous contexts. Do not spend much time on Tier I words, as most students will know them. To assist at-risk learners, ask student volunteers to provide a common synonym for an unfamiliar Tier I word.

Tier II

Tier II words are the words of academic language. Tier II words are found in nonfiction texts across subject areas. They have been referred to as "mortar" words, as they connect different contexts. Students most probably will not hear these words used repeatedly in context, and therefore, will not be familiar with them. These words will appear increasingly in academic texts as students move through the grades and should be explicitly taught.

Tier III

Tier III words are domain-specific words. They are low-frequency words that do not generalize well. Historical and mathematics terms are examples of Tier III words. While Tier III words are important to building knowledge and conceptual understanding within a specific content area, they rarely appear in general usage. Unfortunately, most teacher guides and textbooks focus solely on Tier III words. To build vocabulary, you must decide which words are Tier III words and briefly explain them, but elaborate only when necessary. Excessive exercises or memorization are not often worthwhile for words with a limited range of use.

978-1-4129-5827-1

Context Check

Experts advise that only five to ten words per chapter or unit be selected for explicit vocabulary-building instruction. However, there are many other words within a chapter or unit that require clarification for understanding the material. Fortunately, there are some guidelines in determining which words should be targeted for direct vocabulary study. Many vocabulary experts suggest the following guidelines:

Important Words

Select words that are important to understanding the text. These words may be found directly in the text, or they may not be in the text but are important to understanding the theme.

Useful Words

Choose words with general utility that are likely to be encountered in the future, such as Tier II words.

Unfamiliar or Confusing Words

Consider teaching words or expressions that may need interpretation, such as multiple-meaning words, abstract nuances, idioms, and metaphoric expressions.

Getting Ready

Follow these steps to determine which vocabulary words you will teach during a specific lesson or unit:

1. Select a chapter from a nonfiction text or a novel.

2. Read through the selection and look for difficult words. Find words with which students have had difficulty, such as multisyllabic words.

3. Read the text again. This time, look for figurative language and multiple-meaning words.

4. Use the **Word Selection and Analysis Chart reproducible (page 14)** to list difficult words, multiple-meaning words, and figurative language. Also include the page number of the word or phrase so you can determine how often the word is used and where it is used.

Word Selection and Analysis Chart

NOVEL OR UNIT TITLE: _____

CHAPTER/PAGE NUMBERS: _____

Word	Page Number(s)	Tier I	Tier II	Tier III	Multiple-Meaning or Figurative	Critical to Understanding the Text

5. Analyze the words you listed. Determine which words are common words (Tier I), high-frequency "mortar" words (Tier II), and domain-specific words (Tier III). Also decide if the word is critical to understanding the text. Put a checkmark in the appropriate column. Some words may have checkmarks in more than one column.

6. Choose five to ten words to teach. When selecting Tier II words, focus on vocabulary that can be connected to key themes or ideas in the text and that naturally coincide with discussions and other activities.

Kid-Friendly Definitions, Examples, and Questions

Teachers, not dictionaries, must define new vocabulary for students. A dictionary is often an inappropriate source for students to learn new, unfamiliar vocabulary. Consider the following:

- There are many definitions from which to pick. One has to have a sense of the word to choose the correct definition.

- Reading a definition does not tell how the word is used. Connotation is extremely important.

- Students need numerous examples in context to glean the meaning of a word.

- Dictionary definitions are truncated and contain words that students do not understand.

Once you have selected five to ten words for explicit vocabulary instruction using the Word Selection and Analysis Chart, go through these planning steps before introducing the words:

Step 1: Write a Kid-Friendly Definition (KFD)

First, locate the most common definition from the dictionary. Note difficult, multisyllabic, multiple-meaning, or repetitive words in the dictionary definition. Replace those difficult words with words students already know. Rewrite the definition using words and sentence structure that are easy to understand. Double-check your KFD. Would a younger student understand this definition? If so, then you have probably created a definition that a diverse student body will readily grasp.

Word	Dictionary Definition	KFD
avid	**Enthusiastic** in **pursuit** of an **interest**	Really excited about something you like a lot and do often
cordial	**Warmly receptive** or welcoming	How you act when you are really happy to see someone
scorn	An **emotion** involving **anger** and **disgust**	When you feel mad and really hate something

Step 2: Write Examples

After you have created a KFD, the next step is to write affirmative and negative examples to extend and refine the meaning of the word. The examples you select should be relevant to students' lives. The more familiar the example, the more effective the word learning will be. Use of examples activates background knowledge, which is a critical component of effective learning. Negative examples are effective in narrowing meaning and providing word boundaries.

Word	Affirmative Examples	Negative Examples
avid	I like coffee and drink it a lot. I am an avid coffee drinker.	I hate to clean house. I try to get out of cleaning house whenever I can. I am not an avid house cleaner.
	My dad is an avid Chicago Bears' fan. He has a Bears' license plate, and he watches Bears' football games. He wears the Chicago Bears' colors.	If you avoid reading at all costs, then you are not an avid reader.
	My granddaughter is an avid reader. She reads all the time. She reads in the car. She wants books for presents instead of toys. She loves to read.	If you do not dislike running but are not excited about it either, then you are not an avid runner.

I learned the word "avid" today. If I learn new vocabulary, then I can become an avid reader!

Step 3: Write Yes/No Questions

After you think of examples to present, craft yes/no questions that will get students' brains thinking. Construct questions that reflect students' lives, such as content they are learning at school or information about popular media, bands, or movies. Begin with obvious sentences that incorporate word definitions.

When presenting yes/no questions, be sure to randomly sequence the presentation. Also consider asking a question that is the exact opposite of how students feel about something to provoke a strong reaction and gain their attention.

Question Examples

- *If science is your favorite class and you read science articles often, are you an avid science student?*

- *If you really like country music, play it all the time, and own a lot of country music CDs, are you an avid country music fan?*

- *Does an avid fan of school lunches pick at his or her food and throw most of it away?*

Word Introduction Plan

To help you create KFDs, examples, and questions that will guide your instruction and help students, use the **Word Introduction Plan reproducible (page 15)**.

Teaching Time

After using the Word Introduction Plan, you are ready to present the new words to students. At first, present each word in its natural context when it comes up in lessons. Follow these steps to present a word:

Step 1

Pronounce the word and have students repeat it after you. Call attention to the number of syllables as well as the spelling. Point out any unique orthographic features in the word. You might also wish to complete the "Say It-Write It Sequence" activity (pages 32–35). Use your Word Introduction Plan for Steps 2 through 5.

Step 2

Provide your Kid-Friendly Definition (KFD).

Step 3

Give the three affirmative examples.

Step 4

Give the three negative examples.

Step 5

Ask the yes/no questions that you wrote.

Step 6

Invite students to give their own examples of yes/no questions.

Step 7

Have students record the vocabulary in a Vocabulary Log, such as the one found on page 31.

After you introduce a word for the first time, consider using it for the lessons that follow in Chapters 1–4.

Word Selection and Analysis Chart

NOVEL OR UNIT TITLE: _____

CHAPTER/PAGE NUMBERS: _____

Word	Page Number(s)	Tier I	Tier II	Tier III	Multiple-Meaning or Figurative	Critical to Understanding the Text

Word Introduction Plan

Book or Unit Title	Chapter/Page Numbers

Central Lesson Theme	

Word	Pages

Kid-Friendly Definition (KFD)

KFD Checklist

❑ Words are ones students already know

❑ Words are easy to understand

❑ Succinct definition

❑ Demonstrates typical use of word

Relationship to Central Lesson Theme

Affirmative Examples	Negative Examples
1.	1.
2.	2.
3.	3.

Yes/No Questions

1.

2.

3.

4.

5.

Take Five

Preparing for and Presenting Effective Lessons

When teaching, *how* you teach is just as important as *what* you teach. Research has demonstrated again and again that what the teacher does in the classroom directly affects student learning. Your teaching behaviors and presentation techniques are the catalysts for learning.

The five effective presentation techniques included in this resource are advance organizer, active engagement, scaffolded instruction, ongoing practice, and big ideas.

Advance Organizer

An advance organizer is a verbal "road map" for students, so they know where they are going and why they are going there. While higher achievers can often ferret out a lesson's direction and make connections to previously learned material, at-risk learners must be explicitly told. Disorganized students do not automatically make connections from one segment of a lesson to another.

To help students cognitively organize before a lesson, start each class with a predictable routine. Tell students:

- to get ready for some important information
- what they are going to learn
- why they are going to learn it
- how it is connected to what they have learned before
- what behavior is expected of them
- how you are going to assess their learning

Active Engagement

To retain information, students must be active during all phases of learning. Too often, at-risk students lose focus and interest leaving all the work (and the learning) to the high achievers. Teachers unintentionally feed into this by using the typical "raise your hand before speaking" routine. Fortunately, there are several ways to ensure that all students are engaged. Some of these strategies include:

Unison/Choral Response

All students respond together on your signal. A signal can be visual, such as a hand drop, or auditory, such as a clap. Unison responses are effective for single-word answers. Be sure to allow a few seconds of "think time" between asking the question and requiring a response.

Partner Response

Students work in pairs to formulate and share answers. Critical for vocabulary activities, this technique lowers the risk for students who are less sure of themselves. It is often beneficial to partner a high achiever with a middle achiever and a middle achiever with a low achiever. During the lesson, regularly stop, present a question, and ask partners to share answers before you randomly call on them, giving students an opportunity to think about and rehearse their answers.

Dry-Erase Board Response

At the start of class, provide each student with a small dry-erase board, a dry-erase marker, and a cloth. If small dry-erase boards are not available at your school, cut large plastic sheets obtained from home improvement stores or use recycled lids from large plastic food storage tubs.

At frequent intervals throughout the lesson, ask students to "board" their responses. This action makes students individually accountable for each response, yet it is less threatening than using paper or giving a verbal response. Tour the room to check answers and gauge how much more practice is needed before moving on. You can also provide individual corrective feedback. For example: *You are almost there!* or *The first part of your answer is correct.*

Note: Because each lesson in this book includes active engagement at several points of instruction, an icon is not included for this presentation technique.

Scaffolded Instruction

Scaffolded instruction refers to providing support at each phase of a lesson so students can learn and become secure in a new skill. With adequate instruction and ongoing feedback from a knowing teacher, new knowledge can be gained and internalized. Following are steps for a scaffolded instruction plan.

Step 1: Teacher Modeling (Watch Me Do It)

At the beginning phase or introduction of the skill, demonstrate how to do the activity while telling students what you are doing. This is the "watch me do it" phase. While performing the activity, talk through each step, showing and explaining. Remember the words *show, tell,* and *interact* as a guide to the type of support you should provide at this stage.

Step 2: Teacher and Students Work Together (Do It With Me)

After modeling, work with students while you teach. This is the "do it with me" phase. During this phase, provide support as needed, but gradually withdraw support as students become more proficient. Step in if a student falters and gradually withdraw support.

Step 3: Students Work Independently (On Your Own)

When students are ready to work independently, this is known as the "on your own" phase. During this phase, closely monitor what students are doing. Correct errors immediately to prevent bad habits from forming. This stage is the ideal time to use dry-erase boards. Be sure to observe students' levels of understanding while providing assistance as needed.

Using scaffolded instruction ("watch me do it," "do it with me," "on your own") enables students to get it right from the start. With clear guidance, they avoid mistakes that interfere with learning and keep their self-esteem intact. Sometimes referred to as "errorless learning," scaffolded instruction is often more effective than reteaching.

📖 Ongoing Practice

How often have you learned something only to forget the concept or process because you were not able to apply the skill repeatedly? Perhaps you were able to successfully complete a task once, but three months later, you forgot some of the steps. For most of us, any skill that we do not routinely apply will most likely be forgotten.

Ongoing Practice for At-Risk Learners

At-risk learners, like all of us, need ongoing practice and review. With repeated practice, students can master and retain concepts, vocabulary, information, and skills. Merely presenting information and moving on to the next skill or vocabulary word is insufficient.

At-risk learners often have difficulty integrating new concepts with previously learned information. You can prevent this by constantly reviewing and integrating. Never leave critical information in the past. If information is important for students to know, be sure it is repeated, revisited, and rehearsed throughout the year.

Remember these words as you plan for repeated practice: *Practice must be **sufficient**, **varied**, **distributed**, and **integrated**.* Following are definitions of these words as they relate to ongoing practice:

- sufficient = good quality and enough to ensure mastery

- varied = uses many learning modalities in a variety of student groupings

- distributed = presented in class and as homework

- integrated = presented within the context of content instruction as well as in isolation

A Word About Assessment Without Sufficient Practice

Avoid presenting concepts followed by immediate assessment because sometimes students appear to have obtained mastery when they have not. In such cases, when the skill is tested again at a later time, students may not have the ability to recall or apply the information or skills. Allow plenty of time for review, practice, and integration before assessing a skill.

Big Idea

As you plan your lessons and get ready to employ advance organizer, active engagement, scaffolded instruction, and ongoing practice, think about the most important ideas and skills that you want to instill in your students. Make an effort to streamline what you teach and to focus on critical content.

Critical Streamlining

Critical streamlining is left to you, the teacher, because you know your students best. Do not depend on the curriculum or textbooks, as these might focus on a "succession of forgettable details" (Wallis & Steptoe, 2006) rather than key concepts taught in-depth. Remember that information cannot be retained unless routinely applied. There is simply too much material to be learned at too shallow a depth. At-risk learners cannot begin to master a curriculum that "gallops through a mind-numbing stream of topics and subtopics" (Wallis & Steptoe, 2006).

Lesson Preparation

To effectively teach all students, especially those at risk, trim the content to a manageable amount. Stop galloping and start reflecting. Take stock of the most important big ideas. As you plan lessons, ask yourself these questions:

- If my students only take one idea away from this lesson/unit, what should that be?

- What do I want them to remember ten years from now?

- What am I teaching that has universal application?

- What are the key concepts that I need to cover in-depth?

- How can I relate these key concepts to other lessons I have taught or to other disciplines?

Take Five Summary

By making the Take Five presentation techniques part of your teaching routine, you will have greater impact on your students, especially at-risk learners. Whether you are teaching sixth-grade literature or eighth-grade advanced algebra, world history or plot elements, kindergarten or high school, these instructional behaviors result in more effective teaching and learning.

CHAPTER 1

Extensive Reading Lessons

Comfort Zone

Objective
Students will select books that they can read independently.

 **Big Idea**

Background Information
Estimates indicate that students can acquire and retain two or three words per day through direct, explicit, contextualized instruction. Given a 180-day school year, that comes to 360–540 words per year, a far cry from the vast number of words necessary for adequate vocabulary growth. In addition to direct, explicit instruction of word meanings, you can encourage students to read more. To accomplish this, students must be taught how to select books at their appropriate reading level, avoiding boredom and frustration.

Reading in the "comfort zone" means that students read well enough to understand the text. There are three components to reading in the comfort zone:

- accurate decoding of 95% of the words or better

- knowledge of at least 90% of the words

- comprehension of at least 75% of the words

Frequently, student novels and textbooks are written above the comfort zone of at-risk readers. Therefore, students must be explicitly taught how to select appropriate books while enjoying incentives that encourage them to read.

Materials
- Comfort Zone reproducible
- novels for modeling book selection
- student fiction and nonfiction books of different levels and genres
- high interest, low reading level novels and books

Instructional Sequence

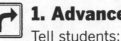 ## 1. Advance Organizer

Tell students:

Heads up for something important! Today you are going to learn how to select books that you can understand and enjoy. To learn the meanings of new words, you must read a lot, but you must read material that is in your personal comfort zone. When you were in elementary school, did you learn a strategy for selecting books? What was that strategy? (Some students might mention the "five-finger rule" or the "three-finger rule.")

Those strategies may have worked well for books that did not have many words on the page, but the books you read now have many more words on the page. I am going to teach you a new strategy in which you will find books in your comfort zone. Everyone's comfort zone will be different. First, I will show you the steps. Then, you will do the steps with me. Finally, you will try them on your own with your leisure reading books. I will check how you're doing by inviting you to read to me.

2. Scaffolded Instruction

Model

Before modeling, give students a copy of the **Comfort Zone reproducible (page 24)**. Go through each step thoroughly and explicitly, thinking aloud and describing what you are doing. Model both positive and negative examples so students are aware that even good readers are selective about what they read.

Modeling Example *The steps of finding your comfort zone are on this sheet. Follow along on the sheet as I show you how to do it. First, I have to pick a book that looks interesting to me. This book looks interesting. John Jakes, one of my favorite authors, wrote it. He writes historical fiction, which is my favorite genre. The title of this book is Charleston. The front cover summarizes the book. So far it looks good, but it has over 500 pages.*

I am going to look through the book at the font and the white space. The font is small, and there are no pictures and not very much white space. I do not think I want to read this book now. It's just too much for me. I am going to try another book.

Do It With Me

Provide a variety of novels for students to examine. It may be necessary to go through this step several times until students are comfortable with the sequence.

Tell students: *I am going to give you a book from the library cart. You each will have a different book. We are going to walk through the "comfort zone" steps together. I will read the step, and you will do what the step says to do.*

On Your Own

Provide time for students to choose and survey a variety of books from the library cart while using the Comfort Zone reproducible as a guide. Tour the room to offer guidance in reading and understanding the steps for choosing a book. Once students choose a book that they feel is in their comfort zone, invite them to read aloud a short excerpt to you. Discuss each student's choice and redirect them if necessary.

Tell students: *Now it's your turn. Take some time with the books and follow the "comfort zone" steps. Ask questions if you do not understand one or more of the steps. When you are ready and have chosen a book, bring it up to me and read part of it aloud. We will talk about whether or not the book seems like a good fit.*

Comfort Zone

Directions: It is important to make sure that a book is in your "comfort zone." If a book is too easy, you will be bored. If a book is too hard, you will be frustrated. Remember, choosing a book that is too hard does not make you a better reader!

> **A book in the COMFORT ZONE means:**
>
> **You can read 98% of the words correctly.**

Here's How to Do It

1. Select a book that seems interesting.
   a. Read the title and front and back covers.
   b. Look at the size of the font, the illustrations, the white space, and the number of pages.
   c. If the book still seems interesting to you, continue with the following steps. If not, choose another book.

2. Choose three sections in the book to test: one near the beginning, one near the middle, and one near the end.

3. Count out about 20 words in the first section, or about three lines of text.

4. "Whisper-read" the passage.

5. Mark any words you have trouble with or do not understand. (Do not count names of people.)

6. Look away from the passage and tell yourself what you just read.

7. If you missed more than one word, the passage was too hard.

8. If you could not explain what the passage was about, the passage was too hard.

9. Repeat Steps 3 through 8 for the middle and the ending sections of the book.

10. If you missed zero to one word in each passage and you could explain each passage, the book is in your comfort zone. Read and enjoy! (If two or more passages are too hard, save the book for later in the year.)

Track It

Objective
Students will read for a required number of minutes per week at their independent reading level.

 **Big Idea**

Background Information
One proven way to improve word knowledge is through extensive reading. In the previous activity, students learned to select books at their reading level. Once students can do this, establish an accountability/incentive system. One incentive is for students to accumulate points for reading books in their comfort zone.

Before You Start
1. Teach students how to select books in their comfort zone. (See pages 21–24.)

2. Ask the librarian to stock the library with a wide range of high-interest, low reading-level books for the range of reading levels.

3. Schedule weekly library time.

4. Enlist the assistance of the librarian and other faculty or staff, and make sure they can help students with finding "comfort zone" books.

Materials
- Track It Reading Log reproducible
- transparency of Track It Reading Log reproducible
- overhead projector

Instructional Sequence

1. Advance Organizer
Tell students:

We will go to the school library every week for you to select or read a book in your comfort zone. You will be expected to read from this book five days per week for at least 20 minutes per day—in or out of class. In order for you to improve your vocabulary and reading ability, you must read, but the books must be in your comfort zone. You will not improve by reading books that are too hard or too easy. You all know that musicians and athletes must practice to get better and perfect their skills. The same is true for reading. You must practice to get better. Think of me as your reading coach.

Each week you will fill out this reading log. I will give you a reading log on (day of week). You must return it by (day of week). You must read for five days for at least 20 consecutive minutes per day. Then you will record what you have read on a reading chart. This chart is worth 100 points. It will be part of your grade in this class. I will monitor you and read your chart each time you turn it in.

2. Scaffolded Instruction

Model

Use an overhead transparency of the **Track It Reading Log reproducible (page 27)** to model how to complete the log. Go through each step, filling in the log exactly as you expect students to do.

Do It With Me

Have students choose a book and read for 20 minutes. Read at the same time as students. Work together to complete one section of the reproducible and sign each student's paper.

3. Ongoing Practice

Have students read in school and at home and mark their progress on the Track It Reading Log reproducible. Check each student's progress once a week and provide rewards when students earn 100 points.

978-1-4129-5827-1

Name _____ Date _____

Track It Reading Log

Day/ Date	Book Title/Pages Read	Start Time/ Stop Time	Total Minutes	Adult's Initials
	Total Minutes This Week			

Student Directions:
- Only "comfort zone" books may be used.
- Tell your parent or an adult that you are starting to read.
- Read 20 minutes or more each day.
- Tell your parent or an adult that you have finished reading for the day. Tell him or her a brief summary of what you read.
- Complete your log and have your parent or an adult sign it.

To Parent/Guardian:

It is critical that your child forms the habit of reading books in his or her comfort zone every day. A book that is too hard will not improve reading, vocabulary, or comprehension skills. The book your child is reading is in his or her comfort zone.

Please encourage your child to read five days per week for at least 20 minutes per session. Each session of 20 minutes or more is worth 20 points. A reading session of less than 20 minutes will not earn any points. Your initials in the last column verify that your child has read for at least 20 minutes and was able to give you a brief summary of what was read.

Thanks for your help!

Weekly Vocabulary Log

Objective

Students will develop independence in vocabulary acquisition by selecting unfamiliar words from their own independent reading.

 **Big Idea**

Background Information

Novice readers have a tendency to skip words that are unfamiliar or that are familiar but have alternate meanings. Typically, at-risk readers struggle so much with decoding that they have little energy left to locate words such as these in reference sources. Thankfully, when students read books in their comfort zone, they can often read with enough fluency to comprehend as well as define unfamiliar words or words that are used in a new context.

Before assigning the following activity, be sure you have taught students how to locate unfamiliar words. The **Vocabulary Log reproducible (page 31)** requires students to locate one vocabulary word for each reading session. This activity is intentionally brief to encourage students to read and locate words without overwhelming them.

Instructional Sequence

 ### 1. Advance Organizer

Tell students:

We are going to begin a daily reading activity to help you look for words that are unfamiliar. To do this, you will record words on a chart. To improve your vocabulary, you must become aware of words that are unfamiliar or familiar words that have meanings that are new to you. You will be locating words on your own in the "comfort zone" books that you are reading.

As you complete your daily 20-minute reading requirement, you should be on the lookout for unusual or unfamiliar words. You will write a word, the page number on which the word appears, the entire sentence that contains the word, and what you think the meaning of the word might be.

Materials

- Vocabulary Log reproducible
- transparency of Vocabulary Log reproducible
- transparencies for several sections from reading selections
- overhead projector

2. Scaffolded Instruction

Model

Before modeling, give students a copy of the Vocabulary Log reproducible. Review the example at the top of the reproducible and explain each element.

Then display a transparency showing a section from a reading selection, such as a novel. Invite students to read the section with you. Use an overhead marker (to simulate a student pencil) to track as you read so students know where to look. When you come to an unusual word, underline it. Be sure to think aloud as you go through the excerpt. Continue to read, underlining unusual words. Call attention to one or two words that are common but used in a unique way.

When you are done, read all the words that you underlined. Choose one word. Replace the reading selection transparency with a Vocabulary Log transparency. Model how to return to the text, locate the word, touch it, say it, and spell it aloud. Return to the chart and write the word as you say the letters aloud. Go back to double-check the word in the text. Complete the chart while thinking aloud.

Do It With Me

Go through the steps another time with a different excerpt. This time ask students to help you with the steps. Repeat with other excerpts to provide additional scaffolding.

On Your Own

During the same instructional session, have students open a comfort zone book. Ask them to work in pairs first to read and jointly select words. Walk around the room, providing assistance as needed. After students have demonstrated mastery working in pairs, have them work independently.

 ### 3. Ongoing Practice

Assign this activity as homework after students have demonstrated mastery working independently under your guidance.

Name _____ Date _____

Vocabulary Log

EXAMPLE
Book Title: *Trapped Between the Lash and the Gun*

Day/Date	Word	Page Number	Exact Sentence
Mon., Jan. 29	pleaded	91	"Do it for me," she <u>pleaded</u>.

Book Title: _____

Day/Date	Word	Page Number	Exact Sentence

CHAPTER 2

Vocabulary Instruction Lessons

Say It-Write It Sequence

Materials
- dry-erase boards

Objective

Students will repeat multisyllabic words, break the words into syllables, and identify spelling patterns.

 **Big Idea**

Background Information

Critical listening skills are key for effective learning in all content areas, especially in speaking, reading, and writing. The lack of critical listening ability especially affects vocabulary and sound-symbol correlation or spelling. To know a word, students must be able to recognize its phonemic features, including the syllables and sounds within each syllable. Often, students with poor vocabulary ability cannot correctly say or repeat multisyllabic words. They have difficulty distinguishing and ordering syllables and the sounds within those syllables. Some students even have difficulty saying all the sounds in words containing consonant blends or clusters.

Phonemic Awareness

The National Reading Panel (2000) found that phonemic awareness is critical to reading success. Not only does awareness of the internal sound structure of words contribute to basic decoding ability, it also affects vocabulary. Knowing what a word means is not only understanding its definition and connotation, but also its phonological form and spelling patterns. In a recent reading study, researchers found that when capable readers encounter an unknown written word, they transfer the word into its spoken components as they attempt to decode and understand it. Therefore, if a student does not recognize the spoken components of the word, he or she will not comprehend the word.

During vocabulary instruction, it is important to call attention to the spoken components of words, specifically syllables, individual sounds, and spelling patterns. Helping students say a word correctly is one of the first steps in helping them improve their vocabulary. Helping students order the syllables and sounds will also help them to spell the word correctly. Both phonological form and orthographic form help students internalize words and improve vocabulary.

Say It-Write It Introduction

To begin the "Say It-Write It Sequence," choose a vocabulary word to introduce based on your advanced lesson planning. Go through all the steps of the "Say It-Write It Sequence" for each new vocabulary word. This gives students many practice opportunities.

All students need practice repeating new words as syllables and then writing the words. Through repeated multisensory practice, students learn the auditory and written properties of vocabulary words. This multisensory practice will help them remember words and recognize words in print.

Once you and your students become familiar with the "Say It-Write It Sequence," the entire routine should take less than one minute. The routine is well worth the effort, as students become critical listeners and learn a strategy for managing multisyllabic words.

Instructional Sequence

 ## 1. Advance Organizer

Tell students:

Get ready for a new vocabulary skill! Whenever we learn a new, unfamiliar, or difficult vocabulary word, we must first pay attention to syllables and individual sounds within those syllables. Knowing syllables and sounds will help you remember the word. Many words sound similar, with only a few sounds that are different. Paying attention to the syllables and the sounds in those syllables will help you learn to read and spell words, too.

On your dry-erase boards, write about a time when you studied syllables. Now write about a time when you studied word sounds. Did you write about learning to read? Did you write about spelling lessons? Both answers are correct. Now we are going to apply what you learned in past years to learning difficult vocabulary words.

Here's how we will do it. Before today, I carefully selected a word when I was making my lesson plans. The word is important for you to know. I will introduce the word in two ways. First, you will say the word syllable by syllable. Then, you will write the word syllable by syllable. After the lesson, I will be looking to see if you can read, write, and say the word correctly.

2. Scaffolded Instruction

Model the Say-It Sequence

Follow these steps to introduce the vocabulary word you have chosen. Explain what a syllable is. Define the word *syllable*. Provide an example of how to identify a syllable. Model the "Say-It Sequence." Say the vocabulary word you are introducing. Say the word syllable by syllable while clapping.

Modeling Example *A **syllable** is the part of a word that has one vowel sound. It is the beat in a word. For example, the word **dog** has one syllable. **Dog** has one vowel sound and one beat, so it gets one clap.* (Say and clap the word dog.)

*The word **injustice** has three vowel sounds. **Injustice** has three beats, so it has three syllables. Listen while I clap out the word **injustice**.* **In** (clap), **jus** (clap), **tis** (clap).

Do It With Me

Once you model the "Say-It Sequence," have students work with you. Say the word in unison. Then say the word alone and say and clap each syllable. Have students repeat the word and clap after you.

Model the Write-It Sequence

Follow these steps to introduce the vocabulary word you have chosen using the "Write-It Sequence." Say the word. Write one scoop for each syllable, leaving enough room for letters to be written inside each scoop. Say each syllable as you write it inside each scoop. Call attention to any orthographic patterns.

Modeling Example *Let's keep working with* **injustice**. *I will make a scoop each time I say a syllable in* **injustice**. **In** *(make a scoop),* **jus** *(make a scoop),* **tice** *(make a scoop). I will touch each scoop, say the syllable, and write the letters.*

Do It With Me

Say the word. Have students repeat it. Guide students to use dry-erase boards to write one scoop for each syllable, leaving enough room for letters to be written inside. Say each syllable as you write the letters inside each scoop. Have students repeat after you.

in   jus   tice

On Your Own

Ask students to erase their boards and repeat the "Write-It Sequence" independently. Circulate around the room and provide redirection as needed.

3. Ongoing Practice

Use the "Say It-Write It Sequence" each time you introduce a new vocabulary word throughout the school year.

Public Record

Objective
Students will record and graph vocabulary words.

 ## Big Idea

Background Information
A basic principle of effective vocabulary instruction is to establish word meaning by providing extensive multisensory exposure to a word in multiple contexts. Researchers have determined that 12 encounters with a word are necessary to place the word firmly in a student's lexicon.

Public Records
In the hustle of daily classroom activity, keeping track of how often words are used can be a challenge. To remedy this, you can keep a public record that is visible to all students and holds everyone accountable for the words.

To create a public record, use chart paper and markers to make a graph like the example on page 37. Write the words in the left-hand column. Each time a word is used, check off the box next to the word. Just by glancing at the chart, it will become apparent which words have been used often and which words need additional practice.

Instructional Sequence

 ### 1. Advance Organizer
Tell students:

In order to remember new vocabulary words, adults and children alike must practice and use a word at least 12 times. In addition to using the dictionary and writing meanings in your Vocabulary Logs, we are going to keep track of vocabulary words. Today we are going to post a graph called a Public Record. Each time I introduce a new word, I am going to write it on this graph. Each time we use a word in a class activity, we will check off a box next to the word.

Our Public Record is a bar graph. You may have used bar graphs in math. Tell a partner when you have used a bar graph and the advantages of using the graph. Who would like to share their ideas with the class?

I expect you to pay attention and remind me when to check off a box next to a word. I will not remind you about any of the words. That's your job! When we have used the word 12 times, you will be expected to know that word. I should be able to give you a test on that word, and you should be able to know the meaning of the word, use the word in a sentence, give an antonym or synonym, and even make an analogy using that word. I will not expect you to know a word until there are 12 boxes checked off. After the twelfth box is checked, it's show time!

 ## 2. Scaffolded Instruction

Model
Post a Public Record chart that you have made. Record five to ten vocabulary words that you chose based on your advance lesson planning. Go through each word, thinking aloud and describing what you will do as students encounter these words in your explicit vocabulary lessons and content area lessons.

Do It With Me
Choose one word and complete the "Say It-Write It Sequence" (pages 32–35). Invite a student to check off one box on the Public Record to show that students have been exposed to the word.

3. Ongoing Practice
Throughout subsequent school days, invite students to remind you when to check off boxes on the graph.

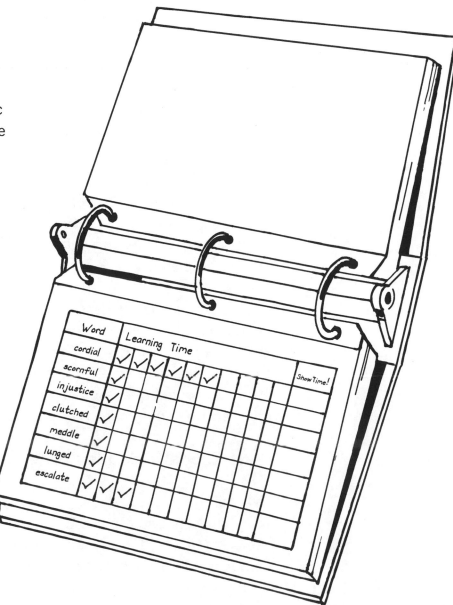

Think, Pair, Share

Objective
Students will process word meanings and create their own connections.

 Big Idea

Background Information
Research consistently indicates that learners understand and remember vocabulary better when they elaborate through speaking and writing. Having students generate their own examples gives them the opportunity to connect words to their own lives. Being able to talk about ideas first with a partner, and then with the whole class, provides opportunities to interact with words as well as with classmates. Students must actively listen to each other and later make judgments about word usage—all keys to internalizing new vocabulary.

Instructional Sequence

1. Advance Organizer
Tell students:

To remember new vocabulary words, you need practice in reading, writing, speaking, and listening to them. Today we are going to play a game called "Think, Pair, Share." You will work with a partner to write and talk about a new vocabulary word that I have chosen for you during my lesson planning.

Let's form partners. Now, tell your partner about a time when you brainstormed original ideas. Was it for a creative writing assignment? Was it for a science experiment? Today you will brainstorm alone and then share your ideas with a partner. We are going to have fun! I expect you to work quietly when you are writing and to listen carefully when you hear your partner's ideas. After today, I will listen for when you use the new word in your speaking and watch for it in your writing.

2. Scaffolded Instruction

Model
Give students a copy of the **Think, Pair, Share reproducible (page 40)**. Guide students to record a vocabulary word that you chose based on your advance lesson planning. Choose a student to help you model the activity while using an overhead transparency of the reproducible.

Materials
- Think, Pair, Share reproducible
- transparency of Think, Pair, Share reproducible
- overhead projector

Think aloud as you complete these steps:

Think Take one minute to think about examples of the word in your life. As you think aloud, write your ideas on the transparency.

Pair Work with a student volunteer for 90 seconds. Together, think of new examples and take turns writing them on the transparency. At the end of the 90 seconds, choose your three most accurate or unique examples by writing the numbers *1*, *2*, and *3* next to your choices.

Share Work with the student volunteer to choose your favorite example. Share it with the class. Have a third student act as the teacher and record the example on the board. Explain that after everyone shares an example, students will write two or three class examples at the bottom of the reproducible.

Do It With Me
Choose a new vocabulary word. Have pairs of students work with you to complete the game, following the steps you described and demonstrated during modeling.

3. Ongoing Practice
Repeat this activity several times during the school year with a variety of student pairings. If you wish, have students bind completed reproducibles into a Think, Pair, Share Journal.

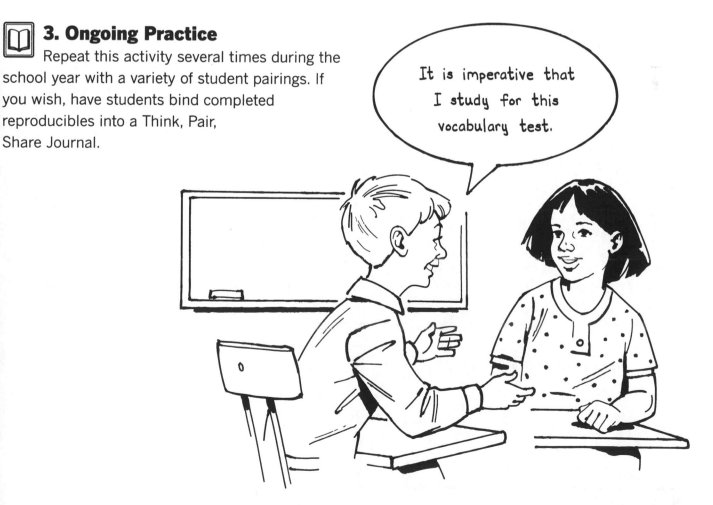

It is imperative that I study for this vocabulary test.

Think, Pair, Share

Vocabulary Word: _____

Think
Think about the word for one minute. Write every example you can think of to show how that word might be used in a sentence.

↓

Pair
Take 90 seconds to talk with a partner about your examples. Write new examples here.

↓

Share
Review the examples with your partner. Rank the three most accurate or unique examples with the numbers *1, 2,* and *3*. Choose a favorite idea to share with the class. Share your idea. Listen as your classmates share. As they list examples similar to yours, write them on this sheet.

↓

Close
Choose two or three good examples from other pairs. Record them here.

Word Structure Map

Objective
Students will make a visual representation that organizes important features of a vocabulary word.

 **Big Idea**

Materials
- Word Structure Map reproducible
- transparency of Word Structure Map reproducible
- overhead projector

Background Information
Graphic organizers are visual representations that provide a framework for remembering important information about a word. A Word Structure Map is a visual representation that organizes important features of the word and provides students a structure with which to think about words. At-risk learners need structure so they can remember, recall, and connect various features of new words.

Instructional Sequence

1. Advance Organizer
Tell students:

When you learn a new word, it is important to understand what it means and how it is used. When you truly understand a word, you can begin to read it, write it, and use it in your everyday speech. Today we are going to use a graphic organizer called a Word Structure Map to learn about new words.

Think about times when you have used graphic organizers. Have you used a KWL chart? Have you made word webs? These are graphic organizers. Today you are going to use a graphic organizer to help you learn new vocabulary.

Today we will complete Word Structure Maps for the first time. After today, we will use them from time to time when we learn new words. Once we complete these maps, I will expect you to know the meanings of the new words, and I will watch for correct usage in your reading and writing.

▦ 2. Scaffolded Instruction

Model

Distribute a **Word Structure Map reproducible (page 44)** to each student. Display a transparency of the reproducible. Demonstrate how to use the map by having students teach you a word that they use every day. Ask a volunteer to offer a word.

Center Box Write the word students choose in the center box. Ask students questions to help you understand the word.

Top Center Box Ask: *What is this word? To what larger category does it belong? Is it an action word? Is it a person, place, or thing? What kind of person, place, or thing? Is it a describing word? If so, what does the word often describe?* Write the word's category in the box.

Right Boxes Ask: *What is this word like? How would you describe this word?* Write three ideas in the boxes down the right side of the page.

Bottom Boxes Ask: *What are some real-life examples of this word? For example, if the word is* **desert***, what are some real-life deserts?* Write three ideas in the boxes along the bottom of the page.

Left Boxes Ask: *What is this word not like?* Write three attributes that ideas that are *not* attributes of the new word and may actually be exact opposites.

Review the completed Word Structure Map with students.

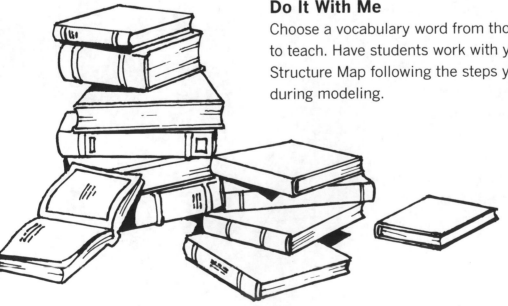

Do It With Me

Choose a vocabulary word from those you have planned to teach. Have students work with you to complete a Word Structure Map following the steps you demonstrated during modeling.

3. Ongoing Practice

Repeat this activity several times during the school year with new vocabulary words. For the first few vocabulary words, model the process. As students become more proficient, ask them to do it with you. After enough practice, students should be able to complete Word Structure Maps in pairs and then share with the class. Once students have demonstrated proficiency with the process, encourage them to ask themselves the four questions from the map whenever they encounter new words in independent reading.

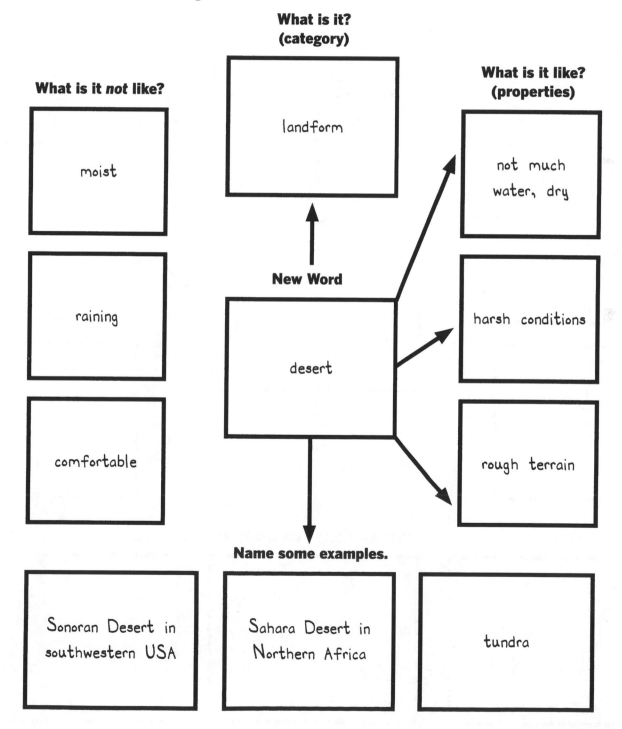

What is it?
(category)

landform

What is it not like?

moist

raining

comfortable

New Word

desert

What is it like?
(properties)

not much water, dry

harsh conditions

rough terrain

Name some examples.

Sonoran Desert in southwestern USA

Sahara Desert in Northern Africa

tundra

Word Structure Map

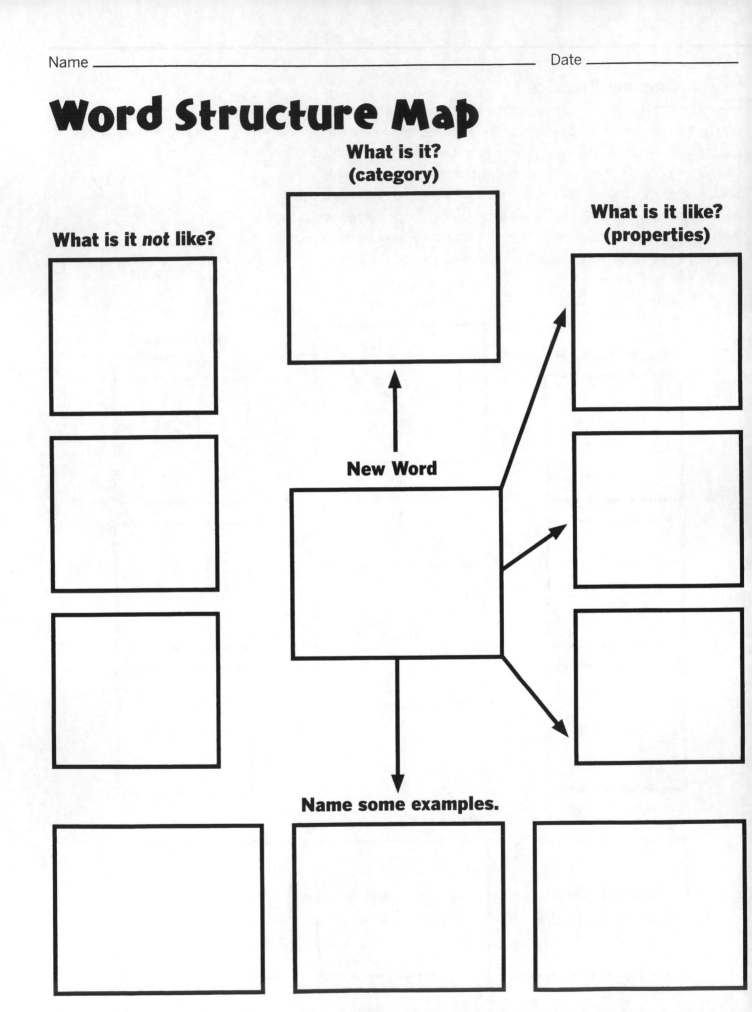

**What is it?
(category)**

What is it *not* like?

**What is it like?
(properties)**

New Word

Name some examples.

The Frayer Model

Objective
Students will use a graphic organizer that provides a framework for remembering important information about a word.

 **Big Idea**

Background Information
Like the Word Structure Map, the Frayer Model is a graphic organizer that provides a framework for remembering important information about a word.

Designed by Dorothy Frayer and colleagues at the University of Wisconsin (Frayer, Frederick, & Klausmeier, 1969), this model uses a four-square format to distinguish the essential characteristics from those only marginally associated with a word. The variation on the traditional model prompts students to think about words in terms of examples, essential characteristics, non-examples, and non-essential characteristics.

Materials
• Frayer Model reproducible
• transparency of Frayer Model reproducible
• overhead projector

Instructional Sequence

1. Advance Organizer
Tell students:

To learn a new word, you must understand what it means and how it is used. When you truly understand a word, you can begin to read it, write it, and use it when you talk. Today we are going to use a new graphic organizer called the Frayer Model. Think about when we used the Word Structure Map. This graphic organizer is somewhat like that map.

Today we will complete the Frayer Model for the first time. After today, we will use it from time to time to learn new words. After some practice, I will expect that you know the meanings of the new words, and I will watch for correct usage.

2. Scaffolded Instruction

Model

Distribute a copy of the **Frayer Model reproducible (page 48)** to each student. Display a transparency of the reproducible. Demonstrate how to use the Frayer Model with a familiar noun.

Center Oval Write the noun in the center oval. Discuss a Kid-Friendly Definition (KFD) and write it under the word.

Bottom Left Box Work with students to brainstorm words or phrases that are examples of the word. Write the examples in the Examples box on the transparency.

Top Left Box Essential characteristics are relevant properties of the word. This may be a difficult concept for students to grasp, especially if the word is not familiar to them. Tell students to look at the examples the class has generated. Ask what all the examples have in common. Write those characteristics in the Essential Characterics box on the transparency.

Bottom Right Box For non-examples, think aloud to generate ideas in the same general category but that are not representative of the target word. For example, if the word is *Eiffel Tower*, you might write *Sears Tower, Empire State Building,* and so on, in the Non-Examples box.

Top Right Box Examine the non-examples and select those characteristics that are irrelevant to the target word. For *Eiffel Tower,* you might write the following non-essential characteristics in the appropiate box on the transparency: *Does not have to be in France. Does not have to be an office building.*

Review the completed Frayer Model with students.

Do It With Me

Choose a vocabulary word from those you have planned to teach. Have students work with you to complete a Frayer Model, following the steps you described and demonstrated during modeling.

3. Ongoing Practice

Use the Frayer Model several times during the school year with new vocabulary words. Model the process the first few times. As students progress, have them complete it with you. After enough practice, have students complete the Frayer Model in groups and then share with the class. Once students have demonstrated proficiency, encourage them to use the Frayer Model mentally when they read new words.

Frayer Model

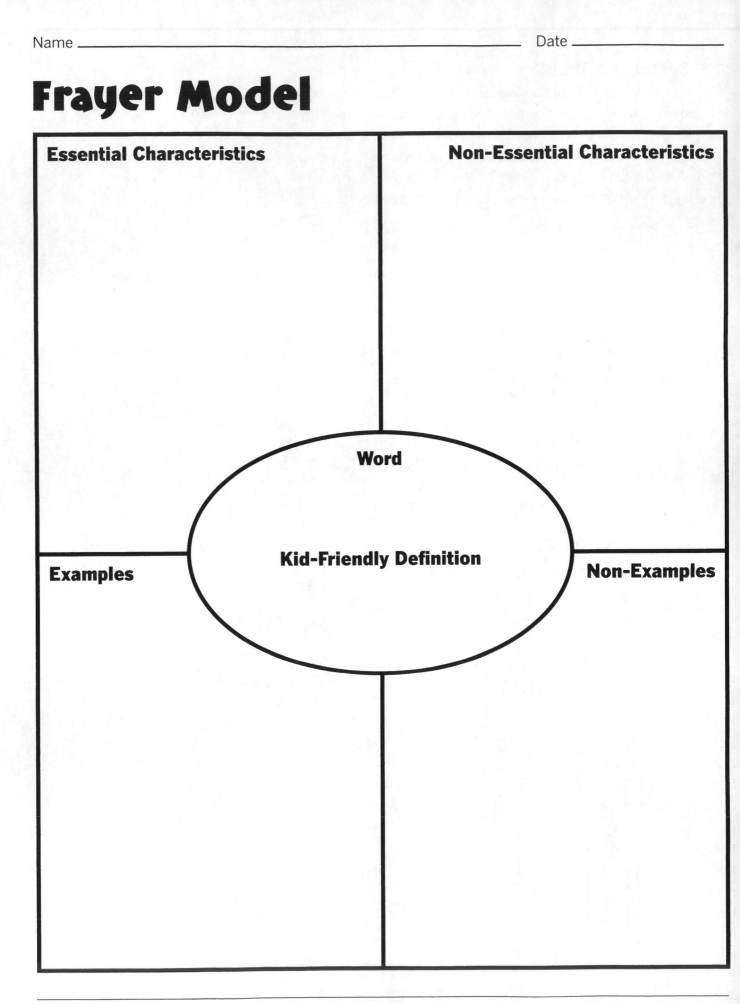

Essential Characteristics

Non-Essential Characteristics

Word

Kid-Friendly Definition

Examples

Non-Examples

Introducing Synonyms and Antonyms

Objective
Students will study synonyms and antonyms to establish and extend vocabulary meaning.

 **Big Idea**

Background Information
Once students are comfortable with the Word Structure Map and the Frayer Model, they are usually ready to work with synonyms and antonyms. Before applying the terms *synonym* and *antonym* to new vocabulary, firmly establish the concepts of *similar* and *opposite*, the meaning of the terms *synonym* and *antonym*, and the variations in word meaning that are acceptable in each category.

To begin, introduce students to synonyms and antonyms in the same lesson to help them become comfortable with the concepts.

Instructional Sequence

1. Advance Organizer
Tell students:

*One good way to learn new vocabulary is to think about how the meaning of a new word is like the meaning of other words. A **synonym** is a word that means the same or almost the same as another word. **Sssssynonym** means **sssssame**.*

*Say the word **synonym** with me. **Synonym** has three syllables. I will clap the syllables for you: **syn** (clap), **o** (clap), **nym** (clap). Repeat the word after me as you clap it out.*

*An **antonym** is a word that means the opposite of another word. Say the word **antonym** with me. **Antonym** has three syllables. I will clap them for you: **ant** (clap), **o** (clap), **nym** (clap). Repeat the word after me as you clap it out. What syllable in the two words is different? (only the first syllable) Which syllables are the same? (the second and third syllables)*

We will work with synonyms and antonyms throughout the year. Once we have had a lot of practice, I will expect you to identify synonyms and antonyms when you read, write, and speak.

Rabbit and Hare

▨ 2. Scaffolded Instruction

Model

Write the word *big* on the chalkboard. Think aloud some synonyms for *big*, such as *huge, large, gigantic, humongous,* and *colossal.* Have students write the words on the board. Repeat with antonyms for *big,* such as *tiny, small, miniscule, wee,* and *microscopic.*

Do It With Me

Invite students to brainstorm with you synonyms for the following words: *fast (swift, speedy, rapid, quick)* and *sad (unhappy, gloomy, depressed).* Repeat with antonyms: *fast (slow, hesitant, plodding)* and *sad (happy, cheerful, gleeful).*

Then teach students how to use a thesaurus to find synonyms and antonyms. Explain: *If you have trouble thinking of synonyms, you can look them up in a thesaurus. Antonyms are often listed, too. You can also use the thesaurus feature on a computer.*

speedy

plodding

3. Ongoing Practice

Gallery Walk

Play "Gallery Walk" to practice the concepts of *synonym* and *antonym*. In advance, make four identical two-column charts on chart paper. Write a vocabulary word as the title for each chart. Write *Synonym* as the left column heading and *Antonym* as the right column heading. Hang the charts in different areas of the classroom.

Organize students into four teams, sending a group to each chart. Provide each team with a different-colored marker. Play with synonyms first. Give each team 30 seconds to brainstorm as many synonyms as they can for the word and record them on their chart. After 30 seconds, have teams rotate to a new chart and add a new synonym for the word on that chart. After 30 seconds, teams must move to the next chart and continue. At each chart, they must try to think of a synonym that hasn't yet been used. Students may use a dictionary, thesaurus, computer, or their notes as they fill in the synonyms. However, they will only have 30 seconds per word to accomplish this task. The word must be written in their team's color.

After several rotations, have students return to their desks. Lead the class in a review of the synonyms created for each word. Teams receive points for words used appropriately, with the highest scoring team designated the winner. As a class, discuss which synonyms are the best matches for the vocabulary words. Put asterisks in front of those words.

Repeat the game using antonym charts and four new teams.

COLD

Synonyms	Antonyms
arctic	boiling
nippy	steaming
shivery	stuffy
bitter	tropical
frozen	hot
frosty	sweltering
snowy	warm
freezing	balmy

Synonym Seekers and Opposites Attract

Objective

Students will apply knowledge of synonyms and antonyms to expand knowledge of vocabulary words.

 **Big Idea**

Background Information

Once students have been introduced to synonyms and antonyms, have them apply their knowledge to new vocabulary. "Synonym Seekers" and "Opposites Attract" are valuable games that help students expand their vocabulary so they can transfer it to reading, writing, and speaking. Once you have made cards for these games, the games can be used repeatedly with no extra work.

Instructional Sequence

1. Advance Organizer

Tell students:

Now that you have been introduced to synonyms and antonyms, we are going to use them to expand our vocabulary. It's important to learn new words so you can become better readers, writers, speakers, and listeners.

You will learn some new words today as we play the games "Synonym Seekers" and "Opposites Attract." Afterward, I will expect you to be able to use the new words when you read, write, and speak. Watch out, these words might even show up on a test!

2. Scaffolded Instruction

Model Synonym Seekers

In advance, record synonym pairs on index cards, one word per card, one card per student. Make one extra synonym pair for modeling. Take one model card. Distribute two other cards to two students, one the model synonym match and one not. Model for students how to walk around the classroom and find your synonym match.

Play the Game

Distribute a card to each student. Have students seek their synonym match. When each student has found his or her match, ask pairs to read aloud their cards for verification.

Model Opposites Attract

In advance, record antonym pairs on index cards, one word per card, one card per student. Make one extra antonym pair for modeling. Take one model card. Distribute two other cards to two students, one the model antonym match and one not. Model for students how to walk around the classroom and find your antonym match.

Play the Game

Distribute a card to each student. Have students seek their antonym match. When each student has found his or her match, ask pairs to read aloud their cards for verification.

3. Ongoing Practice

Play "Synonym Seekers" and "Opposites Attract" throughout the school year, switching out cards and adding new vocabulary as students become proficient at finding matches.

Synonym Analogies

Materials

- Analogy Makers reproducible
- synonym cards from "Synonym Seekers" (page 52)

Objective

Students will study and write synonym analogies.

 **Big Idea**

Background Information

Understanding and writing analogies is an abstract skill and demands several layers of word knowledge and processing. The combination of vocabulary knowledge and logical thinking processes can present challenges for at-risk learners; but with practice, these students can use analogies to develop word knowledge and improve scores on standardized tests.

Instructional Sequence

1. Advance Organizer

Tell students:

It's important to have a lot of practice with synonyms and antonyms so you can learn new words and become better readers, writers, speakers, and listeners. Today we will work with synonyms to make analogies. **Analogies** *are word relationships.*

This is a synonym analogy: **Start** *is to* **begin** *as* **walk** *is to* **stroll***. Analogies are always written in this form. You will often see analogies on standardized tests or reading tests. Raise your hand if you have ever been tested on analogies.*

On a test, your goal in solving an analogy is to find a word that correctly completes the second pair. Sometimes the words in an analogy may seem to have nothing to do with each other, but the words are always logically related. Both pairs of words have the same kind of relationship. To solve the analogy, you need to find that relationship.

Today you are going to write your own synonym analogies. Once you have practiced with synonym analogies, you will work with antonym analogies. Even if I do not give you analogy tests, you must be ready to solve analogies in case you see them on standardized tests.

__Infant__ is to __baby__ as __father__ is to __dad__.

2. Scaffolded Instruction

Model

Write the following words on the board: _Avid_ is to _enthusiatic_. Say, while pointing to the words: **Avid** is related to **enthusiastic** because they are synonyms. Both words mean almost the same thing. The words **is to** mean that **avid** is connected or related to **enthusiastic**.

Say: _There is always a second part to an analogy. This second part has the same logic as the first part—they are sets of words that are connected in the same way._

Write the following to complete the analogy: as _cordial_ is to _polite_. Say: **Cordial** is related or connected to **polite** because they are synonyms. Here's how we say the whole analogy: **Avid** is to **enthusiastic** as **cordial** is to **polite**. Both sets of words are synonyms that are adjectives.

Do It With Me

Give students a copy of the **Analogy Makers reproducible (page 57)**. Work as a class to follow the steps on the reproducible and write three analogies using synonyms. To begin, write _Synonyms_ on the Relationship line.

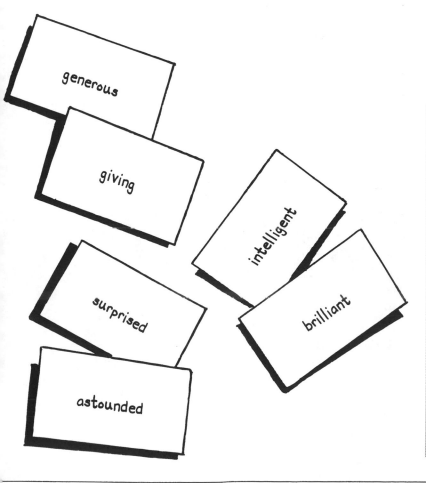

On Your Own

In advance, record synonym pairs on index cards, one word per card, one card per student, or use the synonym cards from "Synonym Seekers" (page 52). Organize pairs of students and provide them with a pair of word cards. Invite each pair to use their words and create an analogy. Ask pairs to record their analogies on the board as classmates record them on their reproducibles.

📖 3. Ongoing Practice

For several days, write the beginning of a synonym analogy on the board before students come to class. For example, you might write: _Boy is to lad as girl is to _____. Have students solve the analogy as they enter class and add it to their Analogy Makers reproducible. Then invite students to write analogies on the board for their classmates to solve as you complete the reproducible again.

Cat is to **kitten** as **dog** is to **puppy**.

Analogy Makers

Directions: To write an analogy:
1. On the Relationship line, write how each word will be related.
2. For your first analogy, write a word in Column 1.
3. Write a related word in Column 2.
4. Choose another word and write it in Column 3.
5. Think about the relationship between Words 1 and 2. Now think of a word that relates to Word 3 in the same way. Write that word in Column 4.

Cat is to kitten as
dog is to puppy.

Relationship: _____

1 Word		2 Related Word	=	3 New Word		4 Related Word
	is to		as		is to	
	is to		as		is to	
	is to		as		is to	
	is to		as		is to	
	is to		as		is to	
	is to		as		is to	
	is to		as		is to	
	is to		as		is to	
	is to		as		is to	
	is to		as		is to	
	is to		as		is to	
	is to		as		is to	
	is to		as		is to	

Antonym Analogies

Objective
Students will study and write antonym analogies.

 **Big Idea**

Background Information
Once students can make analogies with synonyms (pages 54–57), they can work with antonyms to broaden their knowledge and expertise. After playing the "Opposites Attract" game several times, demonstrate for students how to create analogies using opposite relationships. Emphasize that analogies can be created using many relationships, such as cause and effect, part to whole, mathematical reasoning, animal categories, and much more.

Instructional Sequence

1. Advance Organizer
Tell students:

*You know that you need to work with synonyms and antonyms to learn new words and become better readers, writers, speakers, and listeners. You have worked with synonym analogies. Today you will work with antonyms to make analogies. Remember, **analogies** are word relationships.*

*This is an antonym analogy: **Hot** is to **cold** as **thick** is to **thin**. Analogies are always written in this form. I have told you that you will see analogies on standardized tests and reading tests. Have you seen an analogy recently?*

Here is your goal in solving an analogy on a test: Find a word that correctly completes the second pair. Always look for the logical relationship. Both pairs of words have the same kind of relationship. To solve the analogy, you need to find that relationship.

Today you are going to write your own analogies. Even if I do not give you analogy tests, be ready to solve antonym analogies in case you see them on other tests.

<u>**Rough**</u> is to <u>**smooth**</u> as <u>**bent**</u> is to <u>**straight**</u>.

2. Scaffolded Instruction

Model

Write the following words on the board: _Exciting_ is to _boring_. Say, while pointing to the words: **Exciting** is related to **boring** because they are antonyms. The words mean the opposite of each other. The words **is to** mean that **exciting** is connected or related to **boring**.

Say: _There is always a second part to an analogy. This second part has the same logic as the first part—they are sets of words that are connected in the same way._

Write the following to complete the analogy: as _sleepy_ is to _alert_. Say: **Sleepy** is related or connected to **alert** because they are antonyms. Here's how we say the whole analogy: **Exciting** is to **boring** as **sleepy** is to **alert**. Both sets of words are antonyms that are adjectives.

Do It With Me

Give students a copy of the **Analogy Makers reproducible (page 57)**. Work as a class to follow the steps on the reproducible and write three analogies using antonyms. To begin, write _Antonyms_ on the Relationship line.

On Your Own

In advance, write antonyms pairs on index cards, one word per card, one card per student, or use the antonym word cards from "Opposites Attract" (page 53). Organize pairs of students and provide them with a pair of word cards. Invite each pair to use their words and create an analogy. Ask pairs to record their analogies on the board as classmates record them on their reproducibles.

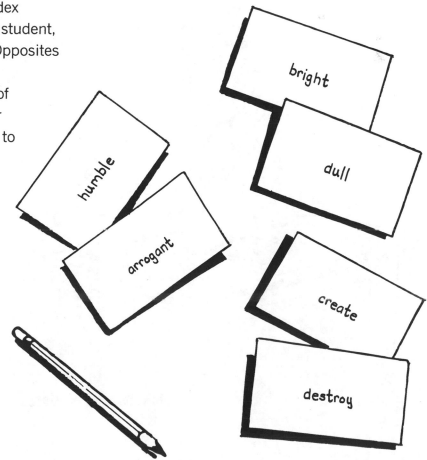

3. Ongoing Practice

For several days, write the beginning of an antonym analogy on the board before students come to class. For example, you might write: _Happy_ is to _sad_ as _good_ is to _____. Have students solve the analogy as they enter class and add it to their Analogy Makers reproducible. Then invite students to write analogies on the board for their classmates to solve as you complete the reproducible again.

Exciting is to **boring** as **sleepy** is to **alert**.

Linear Array

Objective
Students will organize a set of graded synonyms and antonyms.

 **Big Idea**

Background Information
Another activity to do with synonyms and antonyms is the linear array. In a linear array activity, students organize a set of gradable antonyms and synonyms. Gradable synonyms and antonyms can be put on a continuum to indicate degrees of meanings. For example, *gigantic, huge, average, small,* and *tiny* convey a linear array, or scale of size from largest to smallest. Once students identify synonyms and antonyms for target vocabulary through the "Gallery Walk" (page 51), they are ready to scale the words, or put them in a sequence to express degrees of meaning.

("Gallery Walk" (page 51))

Materials
• Linear Arrays reproducible

Instructional Sequence

1. Advance Organizer
Tell students:
Knowing synonyms and antonyms helps you learn many new words so you can become better readers, writers, speakers, and listeners. You have worked with synonym and antonym analogies. Today you will work with synonyms and antonyms to make linear arrays and show how words gradually change meaning.

Think of number lines you have seen in math class. Now think of timelines you have seen in social studies class. Both kinds of lines represent information in an organized, linear way. Today you will work with lines and words.

After you make several linear arrays with new words, I will look for those words in your reading, writing, and speaking. If I or someone else says the words, I will expect you to listen to and understand them.

2. Scaffolded Instruction

Model

Draw a horizontal line on the board with an arrow at either end. Think aloud: *I'm going to brainstorm two synonyms and two antonyms for the word **big**. Here are two synonyms: **huge**, **gargantuan**. Here are two antonyms: **tiny**, **minute**.*

Before writing, model aloud how the words can be sequenced to express degrees of size: target word in the center, synonyms at one end, and antonyms at the other end. Discuss the order of the synonyms and antonyms. Write the words along the array and read them aloud.

gargantuan	huge	big	tiny	minute

←——————————————————————————————————————→

Do It With Me

Give students a copy of the **Linear Arrays reproducible (page 63)**. Point out the lines on the page on which students will make synonym and antonym arrays. Guide students to think about a vocabulary word you chose based on your advance lesson planning. Have students brainstorm two synonyms and two antonyms for the word. Draw another line with two arrows on the board. Have students help you to determine how to arrange the words. Ask questions such as: *Which synonym is closest in meaning to the target vocabulary word? Which antonym is furthest in meaning from the target word?* Write the array on the board as students record it on their reproducible. Repeat with several new words.

On Your Own

Organize students into pairs. Give each pair a list of five words: the target word, two synonyms, and two antonyms. Ask students to create a linear array using the words. As students become more familiar with vocabulary and the process, gradually increase the number of words for them to arrange.

3. Ongoing Practice

Once students become proficient at creating linear arrays, provide them with the target vocabulary word only, allowing them to brainstorm their own synonyms, antonyms, and arrangement. As an extra challenge, provide students with an "extreme" word and ask them to create a linear array working from left to right.

Linear Arrays

Directions: Use these lines to create synonym and antonym arrays.

1.

$\longleftrightarrow$

2.

$\longleftrightarrow$

3.

$\longleftrightarrow$

4.

$\longleftrightarrow$

5.

$\longleftrightarrow$

6.

$\longleftrightarrow$

7.

$\longleftrightarrow$

8.

$\longleftrightarrow$

Show You Know

Objective
Students will write sentences that elaborate on newly learned vocabulary.

 ## Big Idea

Background Information
Using a vocabulary word in a sentence is a typical activity. However, many students, especially at-risk learners, create sentences that tell very little about a new word. They frequently write short sentences such as: *It is scary.* When asked to tell more, they often do not know what to do. Students need specific strategies to create meaningful sentences that expand their understanding of a new word. "Show You Know" is a multi-step strategy for building sentences. This strategy is especially beneficial to English language learners, students with underdeveloped language skills, less prepared students, and others at risk.

Instructional Sequence

1. Advance Organizer
Tell students:

Today you will learn how to write a Show You Know sentence. You will learn to use vocabulary words in complicated sentences and express yourself in a clear, intelligent way.

You have already studied the essential characteristics of many words using the Frayer Model, and you have given some examples of those words. Now you will use what you have learned to create sophisticated sentences.

*Show You Know sentences provide additional information about a word. They can also answer the questions **who**, **when**, **where**, **why**, and **how**.*

Once you have learned to write more sophisticated sentences, I will look for them during creative writing and in essay questions on tests.

▦ 2. Scaffolded Instruction

Model

Display the transparency for the **Show You Know reproducible (page 67)**. Explain that the first task in writing a Show You Know sentence is to think about possible words and phrases that might go with the word. Questions can be helpful to get started. Fill in the transparency, thinking aloud: *I will work with the word* **bleak**. *Even though there are many ways this word can be used, I will concentrate on only one way.*

- **What** *is the word?* **Bleak**.

- **Who** *or* **what** *is bleak? The sky.*

- **When** *might the word occur? During a rainstorm, right before a tornado hits.*

- **Where** *might the word occur? Outside my classroom window.*

- **How** *might the word occur? Suddenly.*

- **Why** *might the word occur? A storm came through.*

Use the phrases to write a sentence. Point out that you will not use all the words in the sentence, but you will try to use those that relate to one another. You may want to have students help you arrange a better sentence. For example, you might write: *One spring day a rainstorm suddenly began and clouds rolled in, changing the blue sky to a bleak, dark gray.*

Do It With Me

After the modeling sentence is completed, have students work with you to be sure it is a Show You Know sentence. Ask: *Is the vocabulary word in the sentence?* Underline the vocabulary word. Ask: *Does the sentence answer these questions? Who or what? When? Where? How? Why?* Underline parts of the sentence as you discuss each question.

On Your Own

Provide students with a copy of the Show You Know reproducible. Ask groups of students to work with a vocabulary word that you have chosen during your lesson planning. Walk the room and provide help as needed.

 ## 3. Ongoing Practice

Repeat this activity several times during the school year with new vocabulary words. For the first few vocabulary words, model the process so students do not forget. After enough practice, students should be able to incorporate Show You Know sentences in their everyday writing.

Show You Know

Directions: Write the vocabulary word. Answer the questions about the word. Write a sentence that uses the word in a meaningful way by including words and phrases from the answers to your questions.

Word: _____

Who or *what* is (the word)?	
When might the word occur?	
Where might the word occur?	
How might the word occur?	
Why might the word occur?	
Show You Know Sentence	

Word: _____

Who or *what* is (the word)?	
When might the word occur?	
Where might the word occur?	
How might the word occur?	
Why might the word occur?	
Show You Know Sentence	

Concept Map

Objective
Students will use a variety of techniques to learn new vocabulary.

 **Big Idea**

Background Information
Once students have explored a variety of word features, such as essential and non-essential characteristics, synonyms and antonyms, and Show You Know sentences, they may be ready to design their own method to remember a word by applying several techniques. In addition to synonyms and antonyms, the nine-square Concept Map includes visual imagery, use of a dictionary, and original sentence writing. Of great use to students with word retrieval deficits, imagery through sketching helps students remember and associate with the word.

Instructional Sequence

 1. Advance Organizer
Tell students:

Today you will study vocabulary words by using synonyms, antonyms, a dictionary, prior knowledge, and even your own drawings. As you think about and study the words by making a Concept Map, you will soon be able to use the words correctly when writing and speaking and understand the words' meanings when reading and listening.

You have already studied the essential characteristics of many words using techniques like the Frayer Model and Show You Know sentences. Now you will combine what you have learned on one Concept Map.

Once you have studied new words and mapped them on a Concept Map, I will look for correct usage in your everyday reading, writing, and speaking. And when I use the words, I will expect that you understand what I am saying.

Interrupt

2. Scaffolded Instruction

Model

Display the transparency for the **Concept Map reproducible (page 70)**. Choose a vocabulary word from your lesson planning. Write the word in the center box.

Beginning at the top left box (Dictionary Definition) and moving left to right and top to bottom, think aloud as you complete the Concept Map for the word.

Do It With Me

Provide students with a copy of the Concept Map reproducible. Guide them to work with a new vocabulary word as you complete the top row of the Concept Map together.

On Your Own

Ask students to complete the middle and bottom rows of the Concept Map on their own. Walk the room and provide help as needed.

3. Ongoing Practice

Repeat this activity several times during the school year with new vocabulary words. For the first few vocabulary words, model one or more Concept Maps so students do not forget. After enough practice, students should be able to complete the Concept Map on their own.

Cordial

Concept Map

Dictionary Definition	Kid-Friendly Definition	Part of Speech
Synonym	**Vocabulary Word** =	**Antonym** ≠
"Show You Know" Sentence	**When might you hear or use this word?**	**Illustrate the word.**

Yes/No/Why

Objective

Students will answer "yes/no/why" questions to interpret and expand word meaning.

 **Big Idea**

Background Information

The "Yes/No/Why" activity is a good way to provide students with an opportunity to make decisions about a word as it changes context. Initially, when creating Kid-Friendly Definitions (KFDs), questions are constructed using words and situations with which students are very familiar. As students begin to hone in on nuances of word meaning, questions can become more complex, using more complicated vocabulary.

   After students have experience with "yes/no" questions, they can be asked to provide a rationale for their answers. These "why" questions can be presented verbally or in writing and can also be used to assess word knowledge.

Instructional Sequence

 ## 1. Advance Organizer

Tell students:

Now that you have had some practice with new vocabulary words, you are ready to think about the words more deeply. Words can have many meanings or one meaning that is used in different ways. It is important to think about all the ways a word might be used, so you can write and speak well and understand true meaning when you read and listen.

   You have already studied the essential characteristics of many words by listening to and writing Kid-Friendly Definitions and answering "yes/ no" questions. Now you will answer "yes/no/why" questions. A "why" question will demonstrate that you understand the "yes/no" questions.

   After this activity, I will look for correct usage in your everyday reading, writing, and speaking. When I say the new words, I will expect that you understand what I am saying.

![icon] 2. Scaffolded Instruction

Model

In advance, choose a vocabulary word from your lesson planning. Model three "yes/no/why" questions that use the new word in the following ways: in an unfamiliar situation, in the context of a current unit of study, and in conjunction with another new vocabulary word. Think aloud your answers as you pose the questions.

For example, if the word is *cordial*, you might model by asking and answering these questions:

- *Will a teacher be cordial to a disruptive student? Why or why not?*

- *Were the Tories cordial to the Patriots? Why or why not?*

- *Is a scornful person often cordial? Why or why not?*

Do It With Me

Choose a new vocabulary word. Work together to generate three "yes/no/why" questions that use the new word in an unfamiliar situation, in the context of a current unit of study, and with another new vocabulary word. Answer the questions together.

On Your Own

Choose a new vocabulary word. Organize students into pairs. Ask pairs to write three "yes/no/why" questions to pose to the class. Remind pairs that they must also write answers to the questions. Have pairs pose their questions to the class and provide answers if the class does not respond correctly.

3. Ongoing Practice

Repeat "yes/no/why" questioning several times during the school year using new vocabulary words.

Word: humble

Unfamiliar Situation	Content Context	With Another New Word
Did medieval peasants often act humble in front of a king or queen?	Was Wilbur a humble pig?	Why might a philanthropist feel humble?

Strategy Lessons

Using Context for Meaning

Objective
Students will learn the steps of using context clues to determine the meaning of unknown vocabulary words.

 **Big Idea**

Background Information
When helping students use context to determine word meaning, be sure to work with text that is within their comfort zone. This is essential because before students can be expected to use context to determine the meaning of unknown words, they must be able to decode and understand at least 90% of the words in a passage, recognize which words they do not understand, and comprehend the majority of the passage.

Keep in mind that teaching context to determine word meaning should not always be the primary focus of vocabulary instruction. Reading researchers agree that solely relying on context to improve vocabulary is often not enough. (Feldman & Kinsella, 2002; Santa, Havens, & Valdes, 2004). Be sure to use other vocabulary strategies in conjunction with using context.

Instructional Sequence

1. Advance Organizer
Tell students:

Sometimes when you are reading, you will come to a word that you do not know. You might be able to use the words and sentences around that word to figure out what the word means. That is called learning from the context. "Using context clues" refers to reading other words and sentences to figure out a word.

You must learn to use context clues because they will help you better understand what you are reading. You have been writing words in a Vocabulary Log. Now you will learn how to use context clues to figure out the meaning of those words.

Be sure to have your Vocabulary Log ready. You will also need the book from which those words came. First, I will show you the steps for using context clues. Next, we will practice. Then, you will use your own books and words for applying context clues. I will expect you to know the steps and to demonstrate the steps when you come to an unknown word.

2. Scaffolded Instruction

Model

Display a Steps for Using Context Clues poster that you made in advance and a transparency of a text selection with a complex vocabulary word. Show, tell, and interact with students as you model the steps for using context clues. Refer to the poster as you work.

Steps for Using Context Clues

1. Underline the unfamiliar word.
2. Read the sentences before and after the word.
3. Paraphrase what you know so far.
4. Summarize what the story is about to this point.
5. Use what you know about the story and the sentence to guess what the word might mean.
6. Read the sentence again and substitute your idea for the word.
7. Decide if the word makes sense.

Modeling Example *This example is an excerpt from* Trapped Between the Lash and the Gun *by Arvella Whitmore. The text selection is:* **Trees stood all around him. Overhead, patches of daylight struggled through tangled branches.**

I can read the word **struggled***, but I do not understand how it is used here. I do not understand how patches of daylight can struggle. I will underline* **struggled***.*

Now I have to read the sentences around that word and think about what they mean: **Trees stood all around him.** *Now I will paraphrase what I know so far. I need to put this in my own words. Since trees are all around him, he must be in some kind of forest. If the branches are tangled, there must be a lot of them all mixed together.*

Now I will summarize and explain what the story is about to this point. At this point in the story, the main character is running away after stealing his grandfather's watch. It is evening. He has ended up in a strange part of town.

I'm going to take a guess at what the word might mean. It is in the evening, so it is getting dark. There are lots of trees and lots of branches. Maybe the word **struggled** *means "had a hard time." When I struggle with something, I have a hard time with it. I will read the sentence again using my idea of the meaning:* **Overhead patches of daylight had a hard time getting through the tangled branches.** *It makes sense that there would not be much daylight because it had a hard time getting through all the mixed-up branches of the trees in the forest. I can picture very little pieces of sunlight coming through to him.*

978-1-4129-5827-1

Do It With Me

Have students help you go through the steps again with a different excerpt. You may want to use several excerpts, including those from students' current studies.

On Your Own

During the same session, have students work independently. Have pairs of students choose a word from their Vocabulary Logs. They should work together through the steps. Walk around the room, providing assistance as needed.

3. Ongoing Practice

Once students are comfortable, you may want to add this activity to their Vocabulary Log time. Start by having students work with one word a week. Gradually work up to all five words, perhaps as a written homework assignment.

Morphology and Meaning

Objective

Students will be able to determine the meaning of words using common prefixes and suffixes.

💡 Big Idea

Background Information

Not all words can be explained from the words and sentences around them. Students also need to know how to use word parts, or morphemes, to figure out what a word means. A *morpheme* is the smallest part of a word that has meaning. Prefixes, suffixes, and word roots are morphemes.

Many struggling readers do not realize that words are made up of parts, nor do they know how prefixes and suffixes can affect the meaning of words. Directly teaching word parts and how to locate them will do much to foster vocabulary growth as well as improve decoding ability.

Initial instruction should focus on morphemes that are clearly recognizable and easily translatable into a meaningful definition. More obscure and less common prefixes, suffixes, and word roots should be taught after students have a firm grasp of the most frequently used morphemes.

anti-

Meaning: against
Examples: antibody, antihero, antioxidant, antiseptic, antiviral, antidote, antitrust, antiwar, anticruelty, antiunion
Antibody: a protein that acts against the antigen in an immune response
Antihero: a "good" guy who lacks heroic qualities

Preparation

Morpheme examples are provided on the **Most Common Prefixes**, **Most Common Suffixes**, and **Common Closed-Syllable Word Roots reproducibles (pages 82–84)**. The morphemes are listed in order of frequency. The first five prefixes, suffixes, and roots should be taught first, followed by the other word parts in order. Alternate between groups using the frequency of reproducibles as a guide. Record the examples on three large posters and display them prominently in the classroom. You might also wish to reproduce the examples and provide them for students to use when they are reading.

In addition to the posters, write prefixes, suffixes, and word roots on large index cards. On the front of each card, write the word part in large black letters. On the back of each card, write the meaning and at least ten examples of words containing this word part. Also provide the definitions for two or three words. Be sure to use different words each time so students have an opportunity to hear and say a wide variety of words. For example, you might write: *inefficient = not efficient, ineffective = not effective, inconvenient = not convenient*.

Color-code the cards for additional cueing, using a different color index card for each of the three parts: prefixes, suffixes, and word roots.

Meaning: state of, condition of
Examples: baldness, happiness, kindness, sadness, softness, calmness, sweetness
Baldness: condition of having no hair
Happiness: state of well-being or contentment

-ness

Instructional Sequence

 1. Advance Organizer

Tell students:

We are going to learn about word parts that add meaning to words. These parts are prefixes, suffixes, and word roots. Learning about word parts can help you learn the meaning of new words. It will also improve your ability to read, write, and speak.

When you are reading and you come across a "big" word that you do not know, you can use context to determine the meaning. But you may also be able to use word parts to break the word into smaller sections to determine what the word means.

*The wall charts I have displayed show word parts that you will learn over several lessons. We will go slowly through the word parts so you can learn them well. You will learn the meaning of each word part, and you will be able to identify the word parts when they appear in text. Today we will work with the prefix **in-**. After all the word parts have been introduced, you will be able to tell the meaning of a word by using its parts.*

2. Scaffolded Instruction

Model

Explain to students that prefixes are word parts that appear at the beginning of words to help give the words meaning. Point to the prefix *in-* on the Most Common Prefixes chart and read it aloud. Display the word card you made. (See Preparation, page 79.) Define this new morpheme. Show the morpheme card and say: *This word part is **in-**. Say it with me: **in-**.* Ask students to repeat the word part. Tell the meaning of the word part: ***In-** means "not."* Have students repeat the meaning of the word part. Ask: *What does **in-** mean?* Have students repeat the meaning of the morpheme.

Provide an oral example such as *incomplete*. Emphasize the word part as you say the word. For example: *Listen while I say a word containing the prefix **in-**; **incomplete**.* Have students repeat the word. Give the meaning of the word using the word and the meaning in a complete sentence: ***Incomplete** means "not complete."*

Then have students repeat the word and the meaning in a complete sentence. Ask: *What does **incomplete** mean?* Students respond: ***Incomplete** means "not complete."*

Say a sentence with *incomplete* using a situation relevant to students: *Here is a sentence using that word: **Christina's homework***

was incomplete, so she did not get credit for it. Then ask students to volunteer sentences using the word *incomplete*. Repeat the activity with several additional spoken words containing *in-*.

Do It With Me

Have students write the word examples containing *in-* as you write them on the board. Say: *Here are the words we just practiced saying. Let's see what they look like in writing.* Have students work with you to circle the word part. Together, go through each word containing the newly introduced word part.

On Your Own

Have students brainstorm and write other words that have the prefix *in-*.

3. Ongoing Practice

Complete the Modeling, Do It With Me, and On Your Own strategies throughout the year with different prefixes, suffixes, and word roots.

As you complete the lessons, add the newly learned morphemes to the card deck. (See Preparation, page 79.) From time to time, go through the word-part deck, showing one part at a time and having students repeat what they read.

You might also wish to create crossword puzzles or fill-in-the-blanks worksheets that feature words containing previously learned word parts. Invite students to circle word parts and/or write the word meanings in the puzzles.

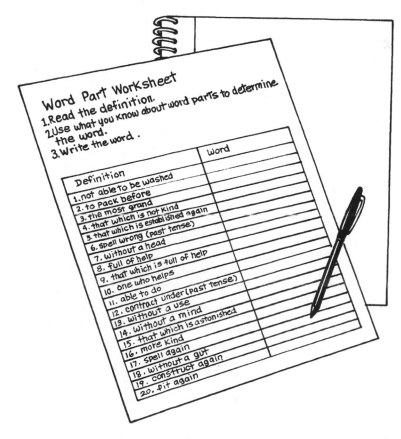

Word Part Worksheet
1. Read the definition.
2. Use what you know about word parts to determine the word.
3. Write the word .

Definition	Word
1. not able to be washed	
2. to pack before	
3. the most grand	
4. that which is not kind	
5. that which is established again	
6. spell wrong (past tense)	
7. without a head	
8. full of help	
9. that which is full of help	
10. one who helps	
11. able to do	
12. contract under (past tense)	
13. without a use	
14. without a mind	
15. that which is astonished	
16. more kind	
17. spell again	
18. without a gut	
19. construct again	
20. fit again	

Most Common Prefixes

Prefix	Meaning	Examples
in-	not	incorrect, injustice
un-	not, opposite of	unhappy, unable
dis-	not, opposite of	distrust, disapprove
mis-	wrongly	misspell, misinterpret
fore-	before	forefather, foretell
re-	again	rethink, reassign
de-	down, away from	deplane, departure
pre-	before	pretest, predetermine
en-, em-	cause to be	enable, embolden
non-	not	nonskid, nonsense
in-, im-	in or into	input, implement
over-	too much	overeat, overextend
sub-	under	subway, submarine
inter-	between	interstate, intercontinental
trans-	across	transatlantic, transport
super-	above	superhero, supersonic
semi-	half	semicircle, semiannual
anti-	against	antiwar, antiseptic
mid-	middle	midday, midsection
under-	too little	underpaid, underweight

All other prefixes (approximately 100) account for only 3% of the total words containing prefixes.

Sources:

Blevins, W. (2001). *Teaching phonics and word study in the intermediate grades.* New York, NY: Scholastic.

Henry, M. (2003). *Unlocking literacy: Effective decoding and spelling instruction.* Baltimore, MD: Paul H. Brookes.

Yoshimoto, R. (1997). Phonemes, phonetics, and phonograms. *Teaching Exceptional Children 29*(3), 43–47.

Most Common Suffixes

Suffix	Meaning	Examples
-s, -es	plural	cats, boxes
-ed	past-tense verbs	jumped, tested
-ing	verbs, present participle	running, laughing
-ly	characteristic of	sadly, friendly
-er, -or	person connected with	jogger, actor
-ion, -tion, -ation, -ition	act or process	action, illumination
-ible, -able	can be done	fixable, hikable
-al, -ial	having characteristics of	formal, cordial
-y	characterized by	bloody, muddy
-ness	state of, condition of	kindness, coldness
-ity, -ty	state of	activity, brevity
-ment	action or process	enjoyment, excitement
-ic	having characteristics of	strategic, allergic
-ous, -eous, -ious	possessing the qualities of	joyous, conscious
-en	made of	golden, wooden
-er	comparative	smaller, tastier
-ive, -ative, -itive	adjective form of noun	active, imaginative
-ful	full of	helpful, handful
-less	without	headless, wireless
-est	comparative	smallest, brightest

All other suffixes (approximately 160) account for only 7% of the total words containing suffixes.

Sources:

Blevins, W. (2001). *Teaching phonics and word study in the intermediate grades.* New York, NY: Scholastic.

Henry, M. (2003). *Unlocking literacy: Effective decoding and spelling instruction.* Baltimore, MD: Paul H. Brookes.

Yoshimoto, R. (1997). Phonemes, phonetics, and phonograms. *Teaching Exceptional Children 29*(3), 43–47.

Common Closed-Syllable Word Roots

Root	Meaning	Examples
scrib, script	write	scribble, scripture
duc, duct	lead	deduce, conduct
spect, spec, spic	to see, watch, observe	speculate, spectrum
mit, mis	send	missile, mission
fac, fact, fic	to make or do	factual, faction
tend, tens, tent	to stretch or strain	tentacle, tendon
cap	to take, catch, seize	capture, captivate
ten, tin	to hold	tension, tenure
sist, stat	stand	static, station
plic	to fold	plicate, plica
struct	build	structure, construct
flact	bend	deflect, reflect
ject	throw	reject, project
rupt	break	rupture, corrupt
gress	to step	progress, congress
vent	come, arrive	ventilate, venture
sect	cut, divide	section, dissect
lect	speak	dialect, lecture
act	do	action, activity
dent	tooth	dental, denture
dict	speak	predict, dictate
fract, frag	break	fragment, fracture
funct	perform, work	defunct, function
junct	join	conjunction, juncture
mand	to order	command, reprimand
opt	eye	optical, optician

Sources:

Blevins, W. (2001). *Teaching phonics and word study in the intermediate grades.* New York, NY: Scholastic.

Henry, M. (2003). *Unlocking literacy: Effective decoding and spelling instruction.* Baltimore, MD: Paul H. Brookes.

Yoshimoto, R. (1997). Phonemes, phonetics, and phonograms. *Teaching Exceptional Children 29*(3), 43–47.

CHAPTER 4

Word Awareness Lessons

Word Power

Objective

Students will increase attentiveness to spoken and written words, locate new words in conversation and reading, and use new words in speaking and writing.

 **Big Idea**

Background Information

A good way to help students develop word awareness and the love of words is through word play. By creating an environment in which word learning is fun, students will be challenged and rewarded. The "Word Power" game was created for just such a purpose. This game has four distinct parts: word nomination, word selection, word use, and word play. All parts work together to effectively build students' vocabularies. At first, it may take an entire class period to introduce all four parts. Once students learn the steps, you will be able to proceed through the four parts effortlessly and incorporate them as a daily activity.

Materials
- Word Power Guidelines reproducible
- Word Power reproducible
- Word Power reproducible copied as a class poster
- dry-erase boards
- gallon bucket labeled *Word Power*
- scrap paper cut into uniform size
- binder
- thesauruses, dictionaries

Instructional Sequence

1. Advance Organizer
Tell students:

Today we are going to learn a game that will increase your vocabulary. Tell a partner what you know about vocabulary. What did your partner tell you? Does anyone have a different idea? **Vocabulary** *means the words you use and can understand when you read or when you hear someone use the words. It is called your* **lexicon***, or the dictionary in your head.*

Use your dry-erase boards to write why you think we need to learn vocabulary. Being able to read is one reason to learn vocabulary. Another reason for learning vocabulary is that it helps you communicate. If you know a variety of words, you will be able to communicate your thoughts more clearly.

We are going to play the "Word Power" game. In this game, you will select the words.

You must listen for the words you use in your daily life. You must pay attention to interesting words. When you hear an interesting word, write it on a piece of scrap paper and put it into the Word Power bucket. Be sure to put your initials on the paper so we know it belongs to you. Each week I will pull one word out of the bucket. I will check to make sure it follows the guidelines. If the word follows the guidelines, I will write it on a Word Power poster. If your word is selected, I will give you some kind of reward. We will go over the specific guidelines in a minute.

Later, we will do a variety of activities with these words. We will play word games and keep track of how you individually use the words.

2. Scaffolded Instruction

Model

In advance, display a large Word Power poster in the classroom, using the **Word Power reproducible (page 91)** as a model. Then model the parts of the "Word Power" game.

Word Nomination and Guidelines Check
Model how to do the word nomination part of the game. Name an interesting word you recently heard or read. Give students a copy of the **Word Power Guidelines reproducible (page 90)**. Say a new vocabulary word and go through the guidelines. Ask: *Does my word meet the guidelines?* If so, write the word on scrap paper and add your initials. Place the word in a Word Power bucket that you place in the front of the room.

Word Selection
Explain that the second part of the Word Power game is word selection. You will select a new word every week. Select your word from the bucket and explain that you will be the only one to read it.

Read the word and have students repeat it. Call attention to the number of syllables and the sounds within the syllables. Then go through the guidelines again to determine if the word is appropriate.

Tell where you heard or read the word. Explain that when you pull a student's word, you will not reveal who nominated it until it has been determined that the word is appropriate. Explain that once a word has been chosen and is deemed an impressive word, the nominating student will get a reward.

Have a few students help you look up the word in a dictionary or a thesaurus. Then read aloud or make up a Kid-Friendly Definition (KFD) for the word.

Give affirmative examples of the word in a sentence and then ask students to provide some as well. For example, if the word is *capricious*, you might say: *What kinds of things would be capricious or very changeable or unpredictable? Well, the weather in Chicago is certainly capricious. Last week the temperatures were in the 60s, and today it is snowing. Chicago's weather is capricious. You never can tell what it's going to be.* Have students think of some examples by either working in pairs or using their dry-erase boards.

Then provide some negative examples of the word and ask students to think of their own. Providing negative examples is critical to clarifying the meaning of the word. For the word *capricious* you might say: *Here is something that is not capricious—the school bell. The bell rings at the same time every day.*

Name the part of speech for the word and use it in an original sentence. For example: *The word **capricious** is an adjective. It tells about a noun. **Weather** is a noun. The **weather** in Chicago is **capricious**.*

Record the word on the class Word Power poster and put your initials next to it to show that it is your word.

Word Use Explain that to expand their vocabularies and make the word truly their own, students need to use the new word and be attentive to its use. Repeated exposure and practice will cement the word in their working vocabularies.

Tell students that they can earn points for using the word in writing; seeing it written in material they read; hearing it used in conversation, on television, or in another class; and using it themselves. Ask them to report word usage during a specified time of the day when you can meet with them individually. After reporting on the use of the word, have students write their initials on the class Word Power poster in the appropriate column. More than one set of initials can appear in each column.

Distribute a copy of the Word Power reproducible to each student. Model how to use the word you nominated and drew from the bucket. Have students write the word on the first line. Then explain each column:

Heard It: *If you hear this word, write your initials in the Heard It column next to the word. You must be able to describe the situation in which you heard the word.*

Said It: *If you claim to have said the word, you must be able to describe the situation in which you said it.*

Read It: *If you read this word, you must show the text in which the word appeared before writing your initials in that column.*

Wrote It: *Before writing your initials in this column, you must produce a piece of writing in which you wrote the word.*

Keep a separate class list of names next to the class Word Power poster. Each time students write their initials on the Word Power poster, they can put a tally mark next to their name. For individual accountability, have students keep track of their own use of the words by putting a tally mark in the appropriate column on individual reproducibles. When a student has marked three tally marks in each section, for a total of 12 marks, that word is closed out. Once a reproducible is filled, students can begin a new one with new words.

Do It With Me

Have the class work together to nominate a word. Go through the process and record the word on the Word Power poster and on students' individual reproducibles.

On Your Own

Invite each student to nominate one word per week. Draw a word from the bucket and add it to the poster if it qualifies. Have students add it to their reproducible and work toward marking 12 tally marks by hearing, saying, reading, or writing the word. Gather students' individual Word Power reproducibles and store them in a binder.

3. Ongoing Practice

The following activities provide engaging ways to play with the words on the Word Power poster. As you use each suggestion, be sure to keep students actively engaged in the process. Have students use dry-erase boards or work with partners. You might wish to turn the activities into a game, awarding the first pair who locates the word a point. Suggest that students find words in the following categories:

- Number of syllables (Example: *Find a word with four syllables.*)

- Types of syllables (Example: *Find a word with an open syllable.*)

- Word parts (Example: *Find a word with the prefix* **un-**.)

- Meanings of word parts (Example: *Find a word with a prefix that means "not."*)

- Spelling conventions (Example: *Find a word in which the* **y** *was changed to* **i** *before the suffix was added.*)

- Definition, synonym, or antonym (Example: *Find a word that is the opposite of* **predictable**.)

- Analogies (Example: **Capricious** *is to* **predictable** *as* **hot** *is to* _____.)

- Words in context (Example: *I can never tell what my granddaughter will like to eat. One day she likes peas, and the next day she hates them. Her food tastes are* _____.)

Word Power Guidelines

Before You Nominate a Word

Make sure that the word:

- is a common noun, an adjective, a verb, or an adverb (no proper nouns).
- is general and not specific to one subject area. (For example, the word *oxygen* would not be appropriate because it likely applies to science only.)
- can be used in writing or speaking by a sixth-grade student.
- can be a replacement (synonym) for a word more commonly used.
- is written legibly on the scrap paper.
- includes your initials next to it.
- has been spell-checked if you have read the word. If you have heard the word, make sure to spell it as accurately as possible.

After the Teacher Writes the Word on the Word Power Poster

Make sure to:

- write your initials next to the word to indicate that you have used it.
- keep a personal record by adding a tally mark next to your name on the class list.
- transfer the information to your reproducible. Write a tally mark on the reproducible to indicate that you have used the word. When a word has earned three tally marks in each section, for a total of 12 marks, that word is closed out. Once your reproducible is filled, you can get a new one.

How You Earn Initials/Tally Marks

If you have done the following with a new word, write it on the poster or reproducible:

Heard It: If you hear this word, write your initials in the Heard It column next to the word. You must be able to describe the situation in which you heard the word.

Said It: If you said the word, you must be able to describe the situation in which you said it.

Read It: If you read the word, you must show the text in which the word appeared before writing your initials.

Wrote It: Before writing your initials in this column, you must produce a piece of writing in which you wrote the word.

Name _____ Date _____

Word Power

Word	Heard It	Said It	Read It	Wrote It
1.				
2.				
3.				
4.				
5.				
6.				
7.				
8.				
9.				
10.				

Word Hunt

Objective
Students will locate unfamiliar, challenging words while they read.

 **Big Idea**

Background Information
Frequently, at-risk learners do not notice unfamiliar words when they read. Sometimes the context gives enough information so the unknown word is not important to comprehension. Students may become so engrossed in a story that they skip the unfamiliar words. At-risk readers need explicit strategies to become more aware of words and take the time to find out what they mean, whether in context, through using reference materials, or through word study. The following lesson helps students increase word awareness while reading so they can develop new vocabulary and become better readers, writers, listeners, and speakers.

Instructional Sequence

 1. Advance Organizer
Tell students:

Today you are going to learn how to pay attention to challenging words that you might skip when you read. Increasing your vocabulary is very important, and the best way to do that is by reading. But you must pay attention to the challenging words. If you skip over them or ignore them, you will miss an opportunity to increase your vocabulary. You also might not understand what you read.

We have worked on challenging vocabulary words before. On your dry-erase boards, write what you think makes a word challenging. For example, a challenging word might be a word that you understand in one context, but not in another.

In the past, I have selected vocabulary words, but this time you are going to find them while you read. You will need to hold a pencil while you read and circle challenging words. After you find the words, you will record them.

After we play "Word Hunt," we will study these vocabulary words in other ways. Once you have read, written, and said the words several times through guided practice, I will expect you to use them correctly every day.

Materials
- Word Hunt reproducible
- current student textbook
- teacher-made Levels of Word Knowledge rating scale poster
- dry-erase boards
- overhead projector and transparency

978-1-4129-5827-1

2. Scaffolded Instruction

Model

In advance, locate a textbook passage that contains a variety of challenging words. These words should be predominately Tier II words. Post a Levels of Word Knowledge rating scale poster that lists the criteria for evaluating word knowledge.

To begin, define what you mean by "challenging words" and tell students how many words you found in the passage that meet this criteria. Do not reveal the words.

Give students a copy of the **Word Hunt reproducible (page 95)**. Explain that they will use this sheet to record challenging words. Model how to read and locate the first challenging word. Hold a pencil and lightly circle the word. Show how to return to the text and record the circled word on the reproducible.

Demonstrate how to write the page number where the word was found and evaluate your level of knowledge using the Levels of Word Knowledge rating scale that you displayed. At this stage, do not define the word.

LEVELS OF WORD KNOWLEDGE

Level 1. I have never seen this word before.

Level 2. I have seen the word, but I do not know what it means.

Level 3. I have an idea what the word might mean, but I never use it. I think it has something to do with (idea).

Level 4. I know the word, and I am comfortable using it.

Do It With Me

Invite students to read the passage with you and find the next challenging word. Have them circle the word and record the information on the Word Hunt reproducible.

Once you have completed the word, page number, and level of understanding for two sample words, work with students to define the words using context clues such as illustrations, photographs, and surrounding words and sentences. Record meanings in the last column on the reproducible. Check the meanings in the textbook's glossary or in a dictionary.

On Your Own

Have students continue reading and recording words, page numbers, and levels of understanding. Ask students to define three or four of the words. Afterward, display your word list on an overhead projector. Read through the words while students consult their papers. Invite volunteers to read aloud the words they defined as classmates record ideas on their reproducibles.

You might wish to award points for each word students found that matches your selection. If a student selects a word that is not on your list and can support why it meets the criteria, you might wish to award double points.

If you would like to determine a winner, have students keep a cumulative point total. The first student to earn a specific number of points is the winner. To reward all students without determining one winner, congratulate all those who meet or exceed the criterion number of points for that chapter.

3. Ongoing Practice

Complete "Word Hunts" throughout the year in several content areas. As you complete the lessons, add the new words to your selection of vocabulary words to study in-depth.

Name _____ Date _____

Word Hunt

Directions:
1. Find a challenging word from the text.
2. Record the word and the page number.
3. Decide on your level of understanding using the Rating Scale Key.
   Write: *1, 2, 3,* or *4*.
4. Write a meaning for the word without using a dictionary. To find the meaning, use context clues: pictures, photos, and words and sentences around the word.

Rating Scale Key
Level 1: I have never seen this word before.
Level 2: I have seen the word, but I do not know what it means.
Level 3: I think I know the word.
Level 4: I know the word!

Word	Page Number	Level of Understanding	Meaning

References

Curtis, M. E., & Long, A. M. (2001). Teaching vocabulary to adolescents to improve comprehension. *Reading Online, 5*(4). Retrieved November 25, 2006, from http://www.readingonline.org/articles/art_index.asp.

Feldman, K., & Kinsella, K. (2002). *Narrowing the gap: The case for explicit vocabulary instruction.* New York, NY: Scholastic, Inc.

Frayer, D., Frederick, W. C., & Klausmeier, H. J. (1969). *A schema for testing the level of concept mastery.* (Working Paper No. 16). Madison, WI: University of Wisconsin.

Henry, M. (2003). *Unlocking literacy: Effective decoding and spelling instruction.* Baltimore, MD: Paul H. Brookes.

Jintendra, A., & Kameenui, E. J. (1994). A review of the concept learning models: Implications for the special education practitioner. *Intervention in School and Clinic, 30*(2), 91–98.

McEwan, E. (2002). *Teach them all to read: Catching the kids who fall through the cracks.* Thousand Oaks, CA: Corwin Press.

Nagy, W., & Anderson, R. C. (1984). How many words are there in printed school English? *Reading Research Quarterly, 19,* 304–330.

National Council of Teachers of English and International Reading Association. (1996). *Standards for the English language arts.* Urbana, IL: National Council of Teachers of English (NCTE).

National Reading Panel. (2000). *Teaching children to read: An evidence-based assessment of the scientific research literature on reading and its implications for reading instruction.* Bethesda, MD: National Institutes of Health.

Santa, C., Havens, L., & Valdes, B. (2004). *Project CRISS: Creating independence through student-owned strategies* (3rd ed.). Dubuque, IA: Kendall/Hunt Publishing Co.

Stahl, S. A. (2003, Spring). *Words are learned incrementally over multiple exposures.* Retrieved November 25, 2006, from the American Educator Web site: http://www.aft.org/pubs-reports/american_educator/spring2003/stahl.html.

Wallis, C., & Steptoe, S. (2006). How to bring our schools out of the 20th century. *Time Magazine, 168*(25), 50–56.